Scaling up Nature-based Solutions to Tackle Water-related Climate Risks

INSIGHTS FROM MEXICO AND THE UNITED KINGDOM

OECD

BETTER POLICIES FOR BETTER LIVES

This work is published under the responsibility of the Secretary-General of the OECD. The opinions expressed and arguments employed herein do not necessarily reflect the official views of OECD member countries.

This document, as well as any data and map included herein, are without prejudice to the status of or sovereignty over any territory, to the delimitation of international frontiers and boundaries and to the name of any territory, city or area.

The statistical data for Israel are supplied by and under the responsibility of the relevant Israeli authorities. The use of such data by the OECD is without prejudice to the status of the Golan Heights, East Jerusalem and Israeli settlements in the West Bank under the terms of international law.

Note by Turkey
The information in this document with reference to "Cyprus" relates to the southern part of the Island. There is no single authority representing both Turkish and Greek Cypriot people on the Island. Turkey recognises the Turkish Republic of Northern Cyprus (TRNC). Until a lasting and equitable solution is found within the context of the United Nations, Turkey shall preserve its position concerning the "Cyprus issue".

Note by all the European Union Member States of the OECD and the European Union
The Republic of Cyprus is recognised by all members of the United Nations with the exception of Turkey. The information in this document relates to the area under the effective control of the Government of the Republic of Cyprus.

Please cite this publication as:
OECD (2021), *Scaling up Nature-based Solutions to Tackle Water-related Climate Risks: Insights from Mexico and the United Kingdom*, OECD Publishing, Paris, *https://doi.org/10.1787/736638c8-en*.

ISBN 978-92-64-58165-4 (print)
ISBN 978-92-64-96669-7 (pdf)

Foreword

Countries around the world have been reeling from the impacts of the COVID-19 crisis. The crisis has been a stark reminder of the vulnerability of economic systems and of people's health to unprecedented shocks. The significant investments now being made as part of national recovery packages present a unique opportunity to build resilience against other global threats of which we are acutely aware, including climate change and biodiversity loss, which significantly undermine nature's capacity to support life as well as future economic development.

Nature-based solutions (NbS), such as riverbed or wetland restoration to reduce flood risk or sand dune restoration to prevent coastal erosion, have come to the fore as measures that can be part of the solutions to address the multiple threats the world is facing and help build resilience to sustain life and economies in the future. Countries have already promoted NbS as part of their international commitments. In the Paris Agreement, NbS are recognised as a way to ensure the "integrity of all ecosystems". The United Nations Convention for Biological Diversity promotes them as a way to tackle the interdependencies between biodiversity loss and climate change. The Sendai Framework supports NbS as a shift away from "grey" disaster protection measures and towards ecosystem-based adaptation.

To seize this opportunity for NbS, countries will need to address some of the obstacles that may have limited their uptake in the past. OECD work has found that NbS were often characterised as being small in scale, pilot projects adopted in ad hoc ways. The time required for their benefits to develop as well as uncertainty regarding their performance in changing environmental conditions have reduced their attractiveness as part of traditional planning and decision-making tools.

This report brings together a unique set of insights from Mexico and the United Kingdom on how we can unleash the potential of NbS to tackle climate risks. It is not enough to promote NbS as part of national biodiversity and climate change strategies and policy priorities. The case studies show that governments have made better use of NbS where the many stakeholders and institutional arrangements that can facilitate NbS were aligned to foster their implementation. Infrastructure and urban development, disaster risk management, and water and forest management are all sectors that drive the implementation of NbS. When regulatory mechanisms, such as land use or building codes, take account of NbS, their use has increased significantly. Traditional "grey" engineering approaches to land use or disaster risk management can be changed by raising awareness, investing in technical capacity and inclusively developing NbS. Regulations, including land-use planning and building codes, play a key facilitating role.

More work is needed. To further enhance the consideration and applicability of NbS in different sectors and their investment decision processes, practitioners need better tools and methodologies to quantify the many co-benefits that can be realised through NbS. The OECD will continue to contribute to these elements in order to harness the full potential of NbS to meet the sustainability challenges our societies and economies will face in the future.

Rodolfo Lacy, Director, Environment Directorate

Acknowledgments

This report was developed by the OECD Environment Directorate, directed by Rodolfo Lacy, and the Climate, Biodiversity and Water Division, led by Simon Buckle. The report was authored by Catherine Gamper, Mikaela Rambali and Brooke Demchuk under the guidance of Xavier Leflaive, Head of the Resilience, Adaptation and Water (RAW) team. The report benefitted from substantive contributions from Lisa Danielson on the policy evaluation framework as well as on the country case studies.

This report would not have been made possible without the commitment and significant contributions from country colleagues who co-ordinated the case study work in Mexico and the United Kingdom, namely Iris Adriana Jimenez Castillo (Secretariat of Environment and Natural Resources) and Bethany Green (Department for Environment, Food and Rural Affairs). The Secretariat is grateful for receiving considerable inputs from a number of different agencies. In Mexico, these included: the National Center for Prevention of Disasters (Centro Nacional de Prevención de Desastres), the National Forestry Commission (Comisión Nacional Forestal), the National Water Commission (Comisión Nacional del Agua), the National Commission of Natural Protected Areas (Comisión Nacional de Áreas Naturales Protegidas), the National Commission of Arid Zones (Comisión Nacional de las Zonas Aridas), the General Directorate of Policies for Climate Change (Dirección General de Políticas para el Cambio Climático), the National Institute of Ecology and Climate Change (Instituto Nacional de Ecología y Cambio Climático), the Ministry of Finance and Public Credit (Secretaría de Hacienda y Crédito Público) and the National Autonomous University of Mexico (Universidad Nacional Autónoma de México). In the United Kingdom, these included: the Department for Environment, Food & Rural Affairs, the Environment Agency, the Forestry Commission, the Knepp Estate, Mott MacDonald, Natural England, the Scottish Environment Protection Agency, the Rivers Trust, the Tweed Forum and the Water Level Management Alliance in the United Kingdom (further details in Annex 2.A and 3.A).

The report benefitted from valuable comments and suggestions throughout a number of iterations from Marta Arbinolo, Helene Blake, Nicolina Lamhauge, Helen Laubenstein, Stephanie Lyons, Michael Mullan, Delia Sanchez Trancon and Edward Perry. Editorial assistance was provided by Jennifer Alain and administrative support from Ines Reale.

The Secretariat would also like to thank the 110 participants for their valuable feedback and suggestions provided during the thematic meeting jointly organised for delegates of the Working Parties on Biodiversity, Water and Ecosystems (WPBWE) and Climate, Investment and Development (WPCID) as well as the Task Force on Climate Change Adaptation (TFCCA) on 3 March 2021.

Table of contents

Tables

Figures

Boxes

Follow OECD Publications on:

http://twitter.com/OECD_Pubs

http://www.facebook.com/OECDPublications

http://www.linkedin.com/groups/OECD-Publications-4645871

http://www.youtube.com/oecdilibrary

http://www.oecd.org/oecddirect/

Abbreviations and acronyms

CENAPRED	National Center for Prevention of Disasters *Centro Nacional de Prevención de Desastres*
CONAFOR	National Forestry Commission *Comisión Nacional Forestal*
CONAGUA	National Water Commission *Comisión Nacional del Agua*
CONANP	National Commission of Natural Protected Areas *Comisión Nacional de Áreas Naturales Protegidas*
CONAZA	National Commission of Arid Zones *Comisión Nacional de las Zonas Aridas*
Defra	Department for Environment, Food & Rural Affairs
DGPCC	General Directorate of Policies for Climate Change *Dirección General de Políticas para el Cambio Climático*
EA	Environment Agency
ECCAP	Climate Change Strategy for Protected Areas *Estrategia de Cambio Climático desde las Áreas Naturales Protegidas*
ENBioMex	National Strategy on Biodiversity and Action Plan *Estrategia Nacional sobre Biodiversidad de México y Plan de Acción*
ENCC	National Strategy on Climate Change *Estrategia Nacional de Cambio Climático*
EU	European Union
FCC	National Climate Change Fund *Fondo para Cuencas Costeras*
FOMIX	Mixed funds CONACYT *Fondos Mixtos del CONACYT*
FONDEN	Natural Disaster Fund *Fondo de Desastres Naturales*
FOPREDEN	Federal Fund for the Prevention of Natural Disasters *Fondo para la Prevencion de Desastres Naturales*
FSIA	Sectorial Fund for Environmental Research SEMARNAT-CONACYT *Fondo Sectorial de Investigación Ambiental de la SEMARNAT y del CONACYT*
GISAMAC	Intersecretarial Group for Health, Food, Environment and Competitiveness *Grupo Intersecretarial de Salud, Alimentación, Medio Ambiente y Competitividad*
IMTA	Mexican Institute of Water Technology *Instituto Mexicano de Tecnología del Agua*
INECC	National Institute of Ecology and Climate Change *Instituto Nacional de Ecología y Cambio Climático*
INPI	National Institute of Indigenous Peoples *Instituto Nacional de los Pueblos Indígenas*
NAP	National adaptation plan
NbS	Nature-based solution
NDC	Nationally determined contribution
NFM	Natural flood management
NGO	Non-governmental organisation

PEF	Budget of Expenditures of the Federation *Presupuesto de Egresos de la Federación*
PNH	National Water Program *Programa Nacional Hídrico*
PNI	National Infrastructure Plan *Programa Nacional de Infraestructura*
POEGT	National General Ecological Spatial Plan *Programa de Ordenamiento Ecológico General del Territorio*
PROECI	Program for the Economic Enhancement of Indigenous Peoples and Communities *Programa para el Fortalecimiento Económico de los Pueblos y Comunidades Indígenas*
Promarnat	Sector Program for the Environment and Natural Resources *Programa Sectorial de Medio Ambiente y Recursos Naturales*
PRONACES	National Strategic Programs of CONACYT *Programas Nacionales Estratégicos del CONACYT*
PROREST	Program for the Protection and Restoration of Ecosystems and Species at Risk *Programa para la Protección y Restauración de Ecosistemas y Especies Prioritarias*
PROSECTUR	Sectoral Program for Tourism 2020-2024 *Programa Sectorial de Turismo*
PSAH	Payment for Hydrological Services Program *Programa de Pago por Servicios Ambientales Hidrológicos*
RMA	Risk management authority
SADER	Ministry of Agriculture and Rural Development *Secretaría de Agricultura y Desarrollo Rural*
SDG	Sustainable Development Goal
SECTUR	Ministry of Tourism *Secretaría de Turismo*
SEDATU	Ministry of Agrarian, Territorial and Urban Development *Secretaría de Desarrollo Agrario, Territorial y Urbano*
SEGOB	Ministry of the Interior *Secretaría de Gobernación*
SEMARNAT	Ministry of Environment and Natural Resources *Secretaría de Medio Ambiente y Recursos Naturales*
SEPA	Scottish Environment Protection Agency
SHCP	Ministry of Finance and Public Credit *Secretaría de Hacienda y Crédito Público*
SNIP	National System of Public Investment *Sistema Nacional de Inversiones*
SuDS	Sustainable drainage system
UNAM	National Autonomous University of Mexico *Universidad Nacional Autónoma de México*
UNFCCC	United Nations Framework Convention on Climate Change

Executive summary

As countries continue to accelerate efforts to mitigate the effects of global warming, adaptation actions remain indispensable to protect communities from the detrimental impacts of climate variability and change. While "grey" engineering solutions, such as dykes or levees, have been the most widely used measures to adapt to and reduce climate risks in the past, nature – and its ecosystem services – has increasingly come to the fore as an effective alternative or complementary solution.

While it takes more time for the full benefits of nature-based solutions (NbS) to be reaped, they have been recognised for the multiple societal challenges they can help to address and the co-benefits they offer. Riverbed or wetland restoration can reduce flood risk and contribute to enhancing biodiversity, while providing sinks for carbon emissions. Their cost efficiency, adaptability to changing environmental conditions (including climate), as well as the multiple co-benefits for human health and well-being have further added to their attractiveness.

In recognition of the effectiveness of NbS in addressing climate risks, a number of international efforts have promoted their use, including the Paris Agreement, the United Nations Convention for Biological Diversity and the Sendai Framework for Disaster Risk Reduction.

For countries to fully exploit the potential of NbS, more knowledge is needed on how to overcome some of the recognised challenges. NbS remain implemented on relatively small scales, and on an ad hoc basis. A lack of awareness and gaps in technical capacity have hindered application at a larger scale. However, major obstacles persist especially in demonstrating (i.e. quantifying) NbS' benefits and performance over time, without which they tend to be outperformed by other solutions.

This report provides insights into country-level efforts, namely from Mexico and the United Kingdom, on how to level the playing field for NbS in the area of water-related climate risks. It structures the discussion around the five dimensions (governance, policies, regulations, technical capacity and finance) that have been identified in previous OECD work as key enabling factors to be considered to scale up the use of NbS.

Key findings and recommendations

Formulating policy targets for NbS can be an effective way to strengthen current policy support

NbS are well-recognised priorities in national climate and biodiversity policies. While their integration into overarching national policies is essential, it is important that sectoral policies (infrastructure, agriculture, water, etc.) include NbS too, as they will ultimately drive their implementation. Considering the trade-offs between NbS and other sectoral policy objectives is important to ensure mutually reinforcing efforts. Finally, the formulation and monitoring of policy targets will be important to strengthen policy effectiveness.

NbS need to be promoted by and co-ordinated among a wide range of actors

Many actors are involved in planning and implementing NbS, including national flood and drought management agencies, public works or infrastructure agencies, infrastructure operators, and regional and local authorities. Other non-governmental actors also play an important role in their uptake. This means that a cross-sectoral and cross-governmental approach is needed. Facilitating collaboration between multiple actors can improve coherence, help create synergies and avoid trade-offs between different policy objectives. Collaboration can also be a starting point to increase ownership and accountability for NbS.

Regulation can unleash considerable opportunities for NbS

Spatial planning determines how housing and infrastructure development and land preservation are envisaged, and hence the role NbS can, and has to, play in that. Given the important role of local governments in spatial planning, countries have issued national guidance and developed tools to help promote the integration of NbS into land-use plans.

Another key regulatory lever that can foster the use of NbS is building codes. More and more countries are working to integrate NbS into building codes, such as requiring a minimum for green space areas on and around new buildings and permeable material in driveways to increase water absorption and retention capacities.

Public procurement is another key regulatory instrument that can determine which specific construction materials or plant species are to be integrated into investments that reduce climate risks. One challenge country practitioners seem to face is the difficulty of demonstrating the full range of the costs and benefits of NbS, which makes it difficult for procurement agencies to follow value-for-money principles.

Information is key to identifying opportunities and triggering action for NbS

To give NbS equal consideration as other solutions, more information is needed about their performance throughout a project's life cycle, considering their maintenance needs and requirements as well as their effectiveness over time when they are applied at a larger scale. There is also a need for this information regarding hybrid solutions (i.e. NbS implemented as a complement to grey infrastructure). Uncertainty around NbS' performance may in turn favour traditionally engineered solutions.

Compiling and communicating increasingly available information on good practices and performance data of NbS, through repositories, guidelines or other design tools, can significantly support the scale at which NbS are used and considered as part of decision-making processes.

NbS face a scattered funding landscape

NbS interventions have distinctive financing needs and standard financing models are not easily adaptable. Until now, NbS have primarily relied on public funding, especially when used as measures to attenuate climate risks for larger areas or communities, i.e. those that have strong public good characteristics.

Funds exclusively dedicated to NbS might exist at the international level (such as dedicated EU funds or funds mobilised through the Global Environment Facility), but the national funding landscape for NbS is usually much more scattered. NbS are supported by environmental protection, climate change or disaster risk reduction funds. Some funds are only gradually making NbS explicitly eligible for funding. However, while NbS may be eligible for certain funds, the difficulty in demonstrating cost effectiveness, and the comparatively high transaction costs, remain an obstacle to obtaining and securing funding over time.

1. Harnessing nature's strengths for addressing water-related climate risks: insights from country experiences

This chapter provides the rationale, international and national policy contexts for the use of nature-based solutions to address water-related climate risks. It summarises the findings of two country case studies in Mexico and the United Kingdom carried out to assess the use of nature-based solutions to date in comparison to the policy objectives the countries set out to achieve. It looks at the potential constraints to scaling up the use of nature-based solutions as well as the opportunities and good practices that are emerging.

1.1. Introduction

1.1.1. The rationale for using nature-based solutions to address the impacts of climate change

Global temperature changes are exacerbating water-related risks with increases in frequency and intensity of heavy precipitation and of drought periods in some regions. A growing body of evidence shows that climate change will intensify the risks of water-related hazards. By creating a warmer lower atmosphere, climate change is altering the water cycle through an increase in evapotranspiration and precipitation and changes to atmospheric and ocean circulation, which can lead to wet regions becoming wetter while dry regions become drier, although there may be regional variations (Masson-Delmotte et al., 2018[1]). Compounding these risks, a deteriorating natural environment worldwide is increasing vulnerability to water-related hazards. Interlinked pressures, such as the loss and degradation of natural areas like wetlands, soil sealing and the densification of built-up areas, are undermining ecosystem functionality (Kabisch et al., 2016[2]). These pressures challenge the provisioning of ecosystem services, such as water retention and water filtration, subsequently affecting human well-being (van der Geest et al., 2019[3]).

While "grey" engineering solutions such as dykes or levees have been the most widely used measures to adapt to and reduce climate risks in the past, nature has increasingly come to the fore as an effective alternative or complementary solution. Riverbed or wetland restoration, for example, are increasingly being considered to reduce flood risk. The multiple co-benefits of nature-based solutions (NbS) have contributed to their increasing attractiveness. Protecting coastal marshes can not only contribute to flood abatement, but it can also enhance carbon and nutrient sequestration and water quality and create a habitat for wildlife and flora (Narayan et al., 2016[4]). Similarily, restoring forests in upper catchments can help to protect communities downstream from flooding, while simultaneously increasing carbon sequestration and protecting biodiversity (Filoso et al., 2017[5]). Finally, NbS have been recognised for their own flexibility and adaptability to changing environmental conditions, including climate change (Chausson et al., 2020[6]).

More recently, evidence on NbS' economic dividends has raised their attractiveness in comparison to grey solutions further. For example, in the north-eastern United States, protected coastal wetlands are estimated to have helped prevent over USD 600 million of direct property damages during Hurricane Sandy (The Nature Conservancy Business Council, 2019[7]). Globally, it is estimated that without mangroves, 15 million more people would suffer from flooding annually (Menéndez et al., 2020[8]). Investments in NbS can stimulate job creation. For example, the American Recovery and Reinvestment Act of 2009 financed coastal habitat restoration projects that yielded an estimated 17 jobs per USD million invested (Edwards, Sutton-Grier and Coyle, 2013[9]). In the European Union (EU), it was estimated that restoring 15% of degraded ecosystems, consistent with Target 2 of the EU 2020 Biodiversity Strategy, would result in between 20 000 and 70 000 full-time jobs (OECD, 2019[10]).

Box 1.1. Defining nature-based solutions

Nature-based solutions (NbS) seek to promote the maintenance, enhancement and restoration of ecosystems as a means to simultaneously address a variety of social, economic and environmental challenges. The International Union for Conservation of Nature coined the term in the early 2000s as "actions to protect, sustainably manage and restore natural or modified ecosystems that address societal challenges effectively and adaptively, simultaneously providing human well-being and biodiversity benefits" (Cohen-Shacham, E et al. (eds), 2016[11]). The European Commission provides a complementary definition and defines NbS as "actions inspired by, supported by or copied from nature and which aim to help societies address a variety of environmental, social and economic challenges in sustainable ways" (Bauduceau, N. et al., 2015[12]). Whereas the International Union for Conservation of Nature definition emphasises the importance of nature conservation and restoration, the European Commission offers a broader perspective and focuses on sustainability in general.

The OECD has approached NbS in its work thus far as measures that protect, sustainably manage or restore nature, with the goal of maintaining or enhancing ecosystem services to address a variety of social, environmental and economic challenges (OECD, 2020[13]). NbS can be considered as an "umbrella concept" for other approaches. For example, the United Kingdom's natural flood management, can be seen as a sub-definition, referring to measures that seek to protect, enhance, emulate or restore the natural function of rivers (EA, 2017[14]). Ecosystem-based adaptation and ecosystem-based disaster risk reduction primarily focus on the use of NbS to address the impacts of climate change. Green or blue infrastructure include either natural or semi-natural features in the development of infrastructure (e.g. green roofs, permeable pavements, retention areas), which can be integrated into the design of housing, airports and other infrastructure developments. They are also often referred to as self-standing measures, such as those used in urban areas (e.g. parks, urban lakes, etc.). It more broadly captures infrastructure that is environmentally friendly.

Source: OECD (2020[13]).

1.1.2. Growing international support for nature-based solutions

A number of international efforts are promoting the use of NbS to help address water-related climate risks. These include the Paris Agreement of the United Nations Framework Convention on Climate Change (UNFCCC), the United Nations Convention for Biological Diversity and the Sendai Framework for Disaster Risk Reduction. The Paris Agreement calls on all Parties to acknowledge "the importance of ensuring the integrity of all ecosystems, including oceans, and the protection of biodiversity, recognised by some cultures as Mother Earth". Parties to the UNFCCC underlined "the essential contribution of nature to addressing climate change and its impacts and the need to address biodiversity loss and climate change in an integrated manner" (UNFCCC, 2020[15]). The Sendai Framework for Disaster Risk Reduction (2015-30) recognises the need to shift from primarily post-disaster planning and recovery to the proactive reduction of risks, and specifies that strategies should consider a range of ecosystem-based solutions. The United Nations Convention for Biological Diversity, at its 14th Conference of the Parties, formally decided to integrate climate change issues into national biodiversity strategies and vice versa, bringing important interdependencies to light (CBD, 2018[16]). NbS efforts for managing climate risks also contribute to meeting other international objectives, such as the Sustainable Development Goals (SDGs), in particular SDG 13 (climate action), SDG 15 (life on land), SDG 6 (clean water) and SDG 14 (life below water). They also contribute to initiatives such the Bonn Challenge on forest and landscape restoration, the New York Declaration on Forests, and to the agenda on land degradation neutrality of the United Nations Convention to Combat Desertification. Similarly, NbS were a priority of the discussions for the G20 Climate

Stewardship Working Group under the G20 Saudi Presidency in 2020 and the United Kingdom is making them one of the priorities of the COP26 Presidency.

International efforts are increasingly mirrored in countries' key national policies. For example, two-thirds of the Paris Agreement signatories refer to NbS as a way to achieve their climate change mitigation or adaptation goals within their nationally determined contributions (NDCs) or their adaptation communications (Seddon et al., 2019[17]). Similarly, 24 out of the 35 OECD countries that have national adaptation plans (NAPs) or strategies explicitly promote the use of NbS for climate adaptation. For example. Australia's NAP highlights the suitability of NbS in the areas of coastal, river as well as urban flooding, while Hungary additionally mentions their effectiveness in mitigating drought risks. NbS are similarly promoted in sectoral policy documents (OECD, 2020[13]) (see Section 1.2). An OECD survey of 27 countries confirms that 23 include NbS in their national water management strategies, the majority of which to promote its use in flood risk management (OECD, 2021[18]).[1]

1.1.3. Early findings suggest that the ambition for using nature-based solutions may not yet be translated into practice

The initial desk review carried out by the OECD suggested that the growing international and national policy ambition to implement NbS has not translated into practice (OECD, 2020[13]). The majority of NbS initiatives have been implemented as one-off projects and in an ad hoc way, often on a pilot basis and on a small-scale. This was confirmed by an OECD survey among water management officials, where only 2 out of the 27 responding countries estimated their implementation of NbS to be in line with stated policy ambitions (OECD, 2021[18]).

The initial OECD review further found that the scaling up of NbS may be constrained by an institutional, regulatory and financial environment that constrains their mainstreaming into the set of solutions used across different sectors. Challenges, such as the lack of awareness and understanding about their performance in the longer run and gaps in technical capacity, hinder the design and implementation of NbS. It also encourages policy makers to turn to options they are used to relying on, especially when they have to take decisions within a short time span. The difficulty of quantifying benefits and the lack of robust performance data make it hard for NbS to be considered on an even playing field with grey solutions. This is further reinforced by a perception that the benefits of NbS are less certain than those of grey solutions (Han and Kuhlicke, 2019[19]; OECD, 2020[13]).

This report uses case studies of Mexico and the United Kingdom to provide insights on how countries are taking action to scale up the use of NbS. The remainder of this chapter summarises the key findings of the case studies to identify common challenges and good practices for scaling up NbS. The case studies provide illustrative examples that may inspire actors to increase leadership, investment and collective action for scaling up the use of NbS.

Future country-focused work by the OECD will enrich these initial findings by incorporating a broader range of experiences, including the use of NbS beyond water-related risks. This includes the use of NbS to address other climate risks (e.g. heatwaves and wildfires) as well as climate change mitigation and safeguarding biodiversity.

1.1.4. Case study methodology

The objectives of the case studies are to understand more concretely and in specific country contexts:

1. the state of play of using NbS
2. the institutional framework
3. the policy context and regulatory framework conditions
4. awareness and technical capacity
5. the funding environment for NbS.

The case studies followed the same process, had the same scope and were guided by the same structure of research questions, as presented below.

Process

A questionnaire (Annex 1.A.) was developed and shared with the main counterparts in each country (namely the Ministry of Environment in Mexico and the Department for Environment, Food & Rural Affairs in the United Kingdom). The country counterparts in turn shared the questionnaires with all of the main governmental stakeholders that are in charge of or contribute to the use of NbS. Questions covered a selection of topics related to each respective country's existing practices, including governance, policies, regulations, technical capacity and finance. Following an analysis of the written responses, consultations of both public and private stakeholders were held in a virtual format in July 2020 for Mexico and in September 2020 for the United Kingdom. These consultations aimed at obtaining complementary information and insights into the more subjective views of policy makers and practitioners to better understand the current practices. A list of the stakeholders who were consulted in each country as well as the questionnaires are available in Annexes 1.A., 2.A. and 3.A.

Scope

NbS can be applied to many policy areas to address societal challenges such as climate change mitigation, biodiversity loss, air and water pollution, or climate change adaptation. In this report, the focus is on the application of NbS for addressing water-related climate risks, which includes measures in the following three areas:

1. **River flooding and urban flooding:** Flood plains, inland wetlands and upland forests can contribute to regulating the flow of water through percolation and topography. Certain natural habitats can also prevent landslides. Similarly, in urban areas, green spaces can reduce flood risks.

2. **Coastal hazards and sea-level rise:** Natural coastal habitats, such as coral reefs, saltmarshes, sea grass or mangroves, can provide effective defences against hazards such as storms and tsunamis as well as from chronic stressors such as sea-level rise and coastal erosion by significantly reducing wave heights and stabilising shorelines.

3. **Water scarcity and droughts:** Natural habitats can contribute to groundwater recharge and to retaining water in soils, while helping to abate soil erosion and drought with moisture absorption. For instance, trees' roots enable them to store and tap into groundwater resources. The water transpires during dry periods, which can be essential for helping ecosystems, farmlands and human communities to cope with drought (FAO, 2019[20]).

The focus on water-related climate risks should render the analysis more comparable and the conclusions and recommendations more relevant to a specific policy community. As mentioned above, in future work, the scope should be expanded to broaden the understanding of the use of NbS in other domains and to strengthen policy support more broadly.

Research questions

The case study work was guided by and builds on the policy evaluation framework developed in the initial OECD policy paper (OECD, 2020[13]). The policy evaluation framework built on an initial assessment of the extent and modality of integrating NbS into existing planning and investment decision-making processes. It supports the identification of bottlenecks and adjustments to existing processes so as to enhance NbS uptake more widely. Applying this framework in the case studies allows going beyond an understanding of barriers to NbS to providing guidance on how these barriers could be overcome to ensure coherent articulation of what NbS can achieve and how they can be deployed at scale.

The policy evaluation framework consists of five dimensions that characterise the enabling environment for NbS for adapting to water-related climate risks in order to overcome the key challenges and that facilitate their uptake: 1) governance arrangements; 2) policies; 3) regulatory requirements; 4) technical capacity; and 5) funding and finance mechanisms (Figure 1.1). These components are critical for facilitating the uptake of NbS by both national and subnational public agencies and private actors.

Figure 1.1. OECD policy evaluation framework for nature-based solutions

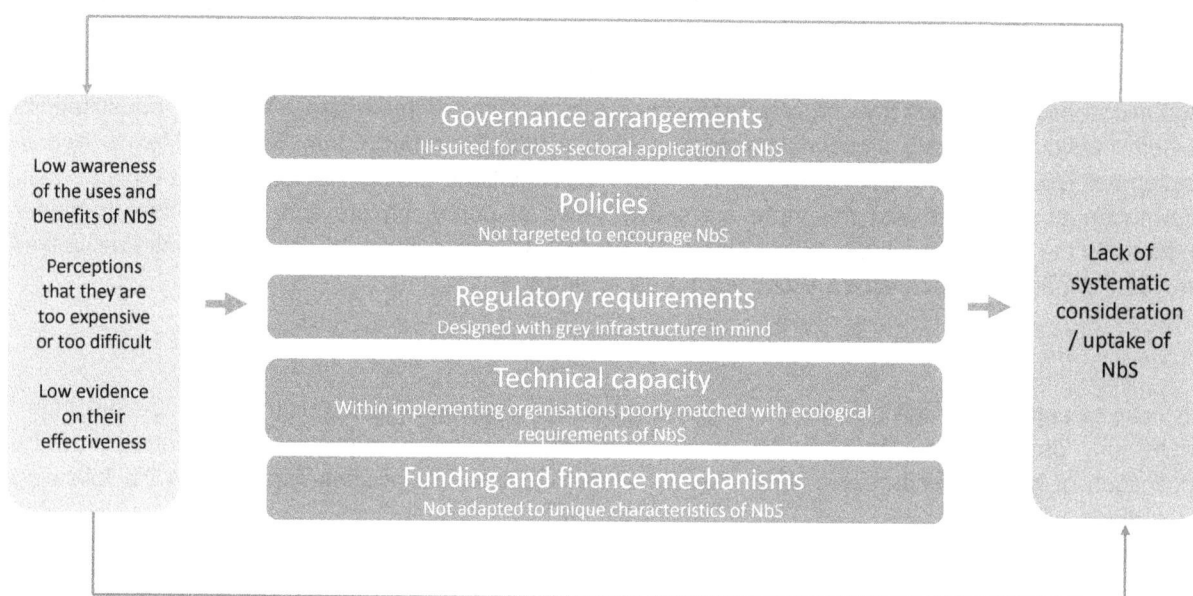

Note: NbS: nature-based solutions.
Source: OECD (2020[13]).

1.1.5. Structure of the report

The remainder of this chapter provides a discussion of the findings from the country case studies, for each dimension of the policy evaluation framework. Chapters 2 and 3 present the detailed case study reports of Mexico and the United Kingdom respectively.

The importance of overarching national and sector-specific policy support

The findings demonstrate that key national policy documents, such as national adaptation plans or the national biodiversity strategies and action plans, have promoted nature-based solutions (NbS) as a means to address climate risks, including those related to water. In addition, NbS feature prominently as both mitigation and adaptation measures in nationally determined contributions (NDCs). More recently, NbS have become part of the measures promoted in COVID-19 recovery packages, such as in New Zealand and the United Kingdom. Although these broader national policies are instrumental in promoting the use of NbS, they need to be mirrored in sectoral policies for policy makers and practitioners to pursue them in the implementation of their sectoral objectives and adequately scaled up (e.g. agriculture, infrastructure, disaster risk management, tourism, etc.).

The findings of the country case studies demonstrate that policy ambitions are rarely tied to concrete targets or monitoring mechanisms, which undermines the policy support.

1.2.1. There is growing policy support for nature-based solutions at the national level

Across OECD countries, NbS are increasingly promoted in key national policies and strategies, notably climate change and biodiversity policies, confirming the initial findings of the OECD report (OECD, 2020[13]). For example, Mexico's Sector Program for Environment and Natural Resources (Programa Sectorial de Medio Ambiente y Recursos Naturales, Promarnat) (2020-24) and its Climate Change Strategy for Protected Areas (Estrategia de Cambio Climático desde las Áreas Naturales Protegidas, ECCAP) (2014-20) heavily emphasise the potential of NbS for adaptation and include concrete actions regarding their implementation (Government of Mexico, 2020[21]; 2017[22]). Mexico and the United Kingdom provide support for NbS in their national biodiversity strategies and action plans. The United Kingdom's strategy promotes the conservation of water ecosystems and encourages natural flood management approaches (Defra, 2011[23]).

In the realm of national policies for climate change, NbS can be found as recommended measures in both adaptation and mitigation plans and strategies. Among the 35 OECD member countries with NAPs, the majority mention the importance of NbS, including, but not exclusively, to address water-related climate risks. Few NAPs include concrete implementation measures, such as the creation of policies or monitoring systems, and no OECD country currently has a NAP that includes quantitative targets related to NbS (OECD, 2020[13]). Mexico and the United Kingdom specifically refer to the importance of NbS in their NAP for managing water-related climate risks, notably for coastal, river and urban flooding. Mexico underlines the potential of ecosystems, notably forests, to moderate the impacts of extreme weather events and the United Kingdom includes ecosystem restoration for adaptation as one of its strategic goals (Government of Mexico, 2016[24]; JNCC and Defra, 2012[25]). Other OECD countries also discuss the role of NbS in their NAPs. Australia underlines the role of NbS to address coastal, riverine and urban flooding and Hungary discusses how well-suited these approaches are for mitigating risk to urban and riverine flooding, as well as drought (OECD, 2020[13]). The EU Strategy on Adaptation to Climate Change also includes NbS as one of its three cross-cutting priorities, with the goal of increasing resilience and contributing to Green Deal objectives. It specifically references NbS measures for reducing flooding, such as wetland and peatland restoration, as well as the potential of NbS in the agriculture sector for adapting to drought (European Commission, 2021[26]).

Similarly, many countries worldwide have included NbS in their NDCs. Although the degree to which NbS are discussed in NDCs varies, the majority of them acknowledge the value of nature and raise the potential of NbS to address both mitigation and adaptation challenges (Seddon et al., 2019[17]). More recently, among those countries that have issued their second NDC, Chile, Colombia and Mexico specifically mention the importance of NbS for adaptation.[2] Chile's updated NDC includes commitments regarding coastal wetlands, peatlands and forests with regard to afforestation, restoration, sustainable management and recovery (Government of Chile, 2020[27]). Mexico emphasises the use of NbS for managing water-related risks, with actions listed including the protection, conservation and restoration of watersheds (Government of Mexico, 2020[28]).

The COVID-19 recovery packages are an opportunity to support NbS as part of a range of measures that will seek to enhance environmental quality. The United Kingdom plans to invest around EUR 30 million through the Green Recovery Challenge Fund that is designed to help environmental groups and public authorities create or safeguard up to 5 000 jobs related to nature conservation and restoration, with a focus on tree planting and the rehabilitation of peatlands. Other countries have employed similar measures, as highlighted in Box 1.2.

1.2.2. Subnational policies increasingly embrace nature-based solutions

Although a comprehensive review has yet to be carried out, there are indications that NbS are increasingly embraced in local level policies. Nearly half of the 210 cities worldwide that had submitted their adaptation plans to the Carbon Disclosure Project in 2016 included measures related to NbS, such as the creation of green spaces for climate change adaptation (UNEP, 2021[29]). NbS investment programmes have accelerated support for NbS at the municipal level too. For example, Manchester's (United Kingdom) Natural Capital Investment Plan specifically encourages investment in NbS projects such as wetland creation and peatland restoration for the purpose of adaptation, supported by the EU Urban Innovation Actions initiative (eftec, Environmental Finance and Countryscape, 2019[30]). More work is needed to decipher how national policy frameworks can inspire and incentivise (and not stifle) subnational initiatives to deploy NbS.

The restoration and conservation of forest and other natural areas, sometimes directly linked to addressing water-related risks, is part of many COVID-19 recovery packages:

- The **EU** Green Deal, presented in 2019, is at the core of the COVID-19 recovery plan. With EUR 750 billion (2021-27) for the Next Generation EU recovery instrument, it aims to protect and restore wetlands, forests, soils and rivers, as well as transform agricultural practices.
- **New Zealand** aims to create over 10 000 jobs with a EUR 650 million programme to invest in actions such as riverbank and wetland restoration.
- **Germany** aims to support efforts such as forest conservation and management, with EUR 700 million of its two-year stimulus package.
- **France** allocated approximately a third of its EUR 100 billion recovery package (2021-22) to accelerating the greening of the economy. Nature is at the core of the measures, which include protecting the coastline and encouraging the agro-ecological transition of agriculture.
- **Finland** dedicated about EUR 53 million in 2020 to protect recreation areas, water services and forest conservation and an additional EUR 13.1 million to rehabilitate natural habitats.
- **Colombia**'s recovery plan includes funding for reforestation and support for sustainable agriculture practices.
- **Chile** plans to have 30% of projects contribute to sustainable, low-emission and resilient development (USD 34 million for 2020-22). It includes afforestation projects, which must be in line with the nationally determined commitments related to forests and biodiversity, notably to help to protect soils, wetlands and water basin sources.

Sources: European Union (2020[31]); Government of New Zealand (2020[32]); Government of Germany (2020[33]); Government of France (2020[34]); Government of Finland (2020[35]); Government of Colombia (2020[36]); Government of Chile (2020[27]).

1.2.3. The integration of nature-based solutions into sectoral policies

While the integration of NbS into overarching and cross-cutting national and subnational policies is essential, it is important that sectoral policies integrate these approaches as well help them gain traction and drive their implementation. With regard to water-related risks, NbS are recognised in many flood and drought management policies, as well as wider water management policies. Indeed, a majority of respondents to a recent OECD survey on water management confirmed that their national water management strategies included NbS (OECD, 2021[18]). In the United Kingdom, for example, natural flood management has been adopted by almost all high-level policies relating to flood risk management, such as the Department for Environment, Food & Rural Affairs' (Defra) Policy Statement on Flood and Coastal Erosion Risk Management, the National Flood and Coastal Erosion Risk Management Strategy for England (2020), and the National Flood and Coastal Erosion Risk Management Strategy for Wales (2020). Mexico's National Water Programme (Programa Nacional Hídrico, PNH) (2020-24) emphasises the potential of NbS for enhancing water security in the context of both floods and droughts (Government of Mexico, 2020[37]). Similarly, in its river basin management plan, Genova (Italy) recommends to opt for "natural techniques [...] whenever possible" to prevent flood and landslides and ensure that soil permeability will not be negatively affected by possible interventions (Hawxwell et al., 2019[38]).

Other important sectors have also started to embrace NbS, for example:

- Agriculture: Updates to the EU Common Agriculture Policy reference measures that fall under the umbrella of NbS, such as the required creation of Ecological Focus Areas by farmers (Underwoord and Tucker, 2016[39]). In addition, the United Kingdom's Agriculture Act 2020 contains specific measures related to the protection and restoration of habitats for the purpose of improving air and water quality, as well as increasing biodiversity net gain (Coe and Finlay, 2020[40]). Mexico's Sectoral Program for Agriculture and Rural Development 2019-24 aims to promote sustainable production, the restoration of ecosystems and adaptation to climate change (OECD, 2020[41]).

- Infrastructure: The UK National Planning Policy Framework goes further by stipulating that new housing and non-residential "developments should only be allowed in areas at risk of flooding where it incorporates sustainable drainage systems, unless there is clear evidence that this would be inappropriate" (MHCLG, 2019[42]). Peru has made advances in mainstreaming NbS into national investment practices, with the public investment programme Invierte.pe explicitly supporting natural infrastructure as part of public infrastructure projects. This opened up financial resources to support the implementation of NbS with USD 300 million of public spending allocated to 209 NbS-related projects in Peru between 2015 and 2018 (OECD, 2020[43]).

Trade-offs are important to consider across policy objectives. For example, NbS for flood risk management, such as the expansion of flood retention areas (used for either temporary or permanent water retention from floods) can have important implications for the use of land for agriculture. They can also have implications for other risks (e.g. increase disease vectors) or for the necessity to convert built land into flood retention areas. Similarly, depending on the context, reforestation and afforestation efforts can affect both nearby and distant water supplies, thereby affecting biodiversity. If efforts focus on monoculture plantations, they risk being more susceptible to wildfires (FAO, 2019[20]). Further work is needed to understand trade-offs and synergies between different policy objectives in order to inform and develop appropriate safeguards to avoid unintended consequences of NbS. These could include, for example, unintentionally generating inequality between local communities or among vulnerable groups and landholders or the overlooking of broader environmental (OECD, 2021[44]).

Data sharing and coordination mechanisms can bring the large number of actors involved in nature-based solutions better together

The planning and implementation of nature-based solutions (NbS) is not the sole responsibility of one government agency. Instead, NbS fall into the mix of tools and measures that can be employed by many actors, including national flood and drought management agencies, public works or infrastructure agencies, infrastructure operators, and regional and local authorities that have significant responsibility. Other non-governmental actors also play an important role in their uptake. This means a cross-sectoral and cross-governmental approach is needed for any effort undertaken to raise awareness or enhance technical capacity, as well as to improve the policy and regulatory environment for NbS.

The findings of the case studies demonstrate that co-ordination in these efforts is needed to ensure that different agencies can converge towards the implementation of NbS. Co-ordination can be operationalised, in a first instance through sharing relevant information between agencies on the use and opportunities for – and co-benefits of – further scaling up NbS.

Local authorities and communities have a key role to play, not only in terms of incorporating NbS into local land-use planning, but also for adapting solutions to local contexts. When local actors are engaged in identifying the potential for NbS and in deciding on solutions that are adapted to their specific contexts, their ownership improves and helps maintain the benefits of the NbS over its life cycle.

Private actors, such as landowners or businesses, can make an important contribution to the use of NbS. In the absence of performance data and of awareness around NbS, the case studies show that public funding instruments can play an important incentivising role to increase the use of NbS and generate financial contributions from the private sector.

1.3.1. Multiple actors and stakeholders are involved in planning and implementing nature-based solutions

NbS planning and implementation involve a wide range of actors from different agencies and non-governmental entities, across different jurisdictions at national and subnational levels. With regard to water-related risks, actors at the central government level are often responsible for driving NbS-related policies and projects. These include flood and drought management agencies, alongside other agencies within environmental ministries, such as those responsible for promoting biodiversity or forest management units.

In both Mexico and the United Kingdom, national agencies in charge of flood and drought management play a key role in shaping policies, providing financial support for NbS projects, and bringing a national strategic role on flood and drought risks to the local issues. The Ministry of Environment and Natural Resources (Secretaría de Medio Ambiente y Recursos Naturales, SEMARNAT) in Mexico and Defra in the United Kingdom actively promote NbS for water-related climate risks through their policies on water resources, including flooding, coastal erosion and drought. These actors, who have taken increased ownership of NbS, are mainstreaming them into their decision-making processes and finance mechanisms (e.g. by making NbS eligible for funding through water and environmental management programmes).

At the subnational level, regional and municipal authorities are important drivers of NbS planning and implementation. They can incentivise NbS through regulations: in Mexico, regional and municipal authorities have an instrumental role in defining land use and regulations, including environmental permitting. They also drive implementation, like in the United Kingdom, where subnational authorities, such as local authorities or internal drainage boards, are tasked to carry out projects. Although no NbS-specific vertical co-ordination mechanisms exist across levels of administration in Mexico or the United Kingdom, subnational authorities co-ordinate through funding mechanisms. For instance, Defra provides national co-funding to flood and coastal erosion management projects, complemented by local sources of funding (e.g. through grant-in-aid, discussed in more detail below).

Other non-governmental stakeholders have important roles in the implementation of NbS. These include infrastructure operators, such as water utilities that might incorporate NbS into their operations. Private businesses may increasingly consider NbS as part of their operations as well. Non-governmental organisations may integrate NbS as part of their activities and promote them as part of their environmental objectives. Private landowners (such as farmers) and indigenous peoples with land rights can also play an active role if their land is to be dedicated to NbS. In practice, it has been shown that while it may take time to convince farmers, for example, of the value of NbS in the beginning, they have become strong supporters when once they have experienced the benefits yielded by NbS, such as with regard to soil quality or the water storage capacity of their land. The UK government worked with the Royal Society for the Protection of Birds and other partners, such as the company Crossrail, on the Wallasea Island (United Kingdom) to control water levels and create a variety of depths of water to suit different species by managing saline lagoons (RSPB, n.d.[45]).

1.3.2. Co-ordination across governmental agencies

Co-ordination among governmental agencies is important to foster coherence and synergies across policies and initiatives relevant for NbS and to address trade-offs between them, where necessary. Co-ordination is further needed, as NbS planning and implementation build on regulations and policies that go beyond a single agency's responsibility or jurisdiction.

When central government agencies operate in silos, with their own visions and objectives, legal frameworks, planning documents, resources and procedures, it is more difficult to incentivise collaboration or facilitate the implementation of NbS. To overcome this, some good practices are emerging. Agencies, such as the UK Environment Agency, which steers flood risk management across England, play an important co-ordination role both with other government agencies as well as with non-state actors. They have played a key role in the dialogue with actors to raise awareness about NbS and to accompany them and address concerns in the process of implementing NbS, such as shown in the above example of working with farmers. As part of an EU Horizon 2020 project, a polycentric governance approach was established to restore a section of the Isar River (Munich, Germany) to increase flood protection, recreational potential and improve ecological quality. This collaboration was facilitated by a cross-sectoral work group, which cut across the silos of water and urban planning, involving multiple institutional scales and sectors (European Commission, 2020[46]). As part of its efforts to develop a long-term vision on cross-cutting issues for the Chilean Long Term Strategy, Chile is undertaking a participatory process focusing on the role of ecosystem functions and NbS.

Co-ordination can be operationalised through data and knowledge sharing between agencies. However, countries do not necessarily have specific mechanisms, such as an exchange platform, in place to facilitate this. Sometimes public bodies, such as in Mexico, have their own platforms for hosting information, making it difficult for practitioners to access the information necessary for a project. Co-ordination can occur through cross-agency financing of NbS (see below).

1.3.3. Co-ordination and engagement with non-state actors

The co-ordination and engagement between governmental and non-governmental actors can occur at different stages of the process, from planning to financing and implementing NbS interventions. A number of examples of collaboration exist. For instance, the UK Environment Agency, in collaboration with the Royal Society for the Protection of Birds, engineers and the local community, created a coastal wetland at Medmerry (South England) to address coastal climate hazards and reduce flood risk for over 300 homes. Local communities were engaged in the design process to ensure that the wetland enhanced recreational opportunities (RSPB, 2015[47]). A study of close to 1 000 NbS initiatives in European cities shows that a majority of projects are jointly led by public and non-governmental actors (European Commission, 2020[46]). Collaboration between those actors enables them to learn from each other, exchange information about new designs, and account for various needs and perceptions from different perspectives. In the city of Antwerp (Belgium), a co-creation process engaged citizens, urban planners and designers to help set up a green corridor to connect different NbS for water retention and foster resilience, building on a diversity of approaches and social innovation (Frantzeskaki, 2019[48]).

The government is also encouraging private actors to contribute to funding projects, providing financial incentives that can mobilise various stakeholders in NbS implementation. Financial instruments such as the land stewardship scheme[3] in the United Kingdom or payment for ecosystem services schemes in Mexico help to engage with private actors on NbS projects. As part of the Payment for Hydrological Services Programme (Programa de Pago por Servicios Ambientales Hidrológicos, PSAH), forest communities in Mexico can be paid for conserving land.

1.3.4. Ownership and accountability is important for sustaining the benefits of nature-based solutions over time

Long-term ownership of and accountability for NbS is important to ensure that they maintain their benefits over time. While it is increasingly clear who initiates and implements them, long-term responsibilities can be blurred. This has been raised as a challenge in the United Kingdom, especially when it comes to identifying who is liable for the long-term maintenance and sustained performance of NbS over time. Clear distribution of roles and responsibilities, backed by resources to support longer term efforts, is therefore important.

Ownership can also pose issues, where specific NbS interventions benefit more actors than the ones responsible for implementing and maintaining them. In the United Kingdom, much of the land is owned privately, which requires an engagement with landowners to best define possible compensation for using the land (OECD, 2021[49]). For example, the land used for riverbed or watershed restoration by an individual land owner may provide flood risk reduction benefits for other land owners nearby. These issues can arise, for example, at watershed scales or where NbS connect upstream and downstream, rural and urban areas. NbS benefits spill over beyond the jurisdiction that implements them. Equity issues may also arise over time, meaning that the governance settings might have to reflect changing needs of the people who manage and rely on these ecosystems.

Regulatory reform can unleash considerable opportunities for nature-based solutions

Adjusting spatial planning, which shapes the location and design of interventions, to better integrate nature-based solutions (NbS) can help better address water-related climate risks. Planning determines the areas where new building and infrastructure development can take place, and under which conditions. Local communities play a critical role in spatial planning, and in recognition of this, countries have issued national guidance and developed tools to help promote the consideration of NbS at the local level.

Another key regulatory lever that can foster the use of NbS is building codes, which fall equally often under local jurisdictions. Building codes include legal prescriptions of the material and design to be used to address water-related risks. In recent and ongoing building code reforms, more and more countries are working to integrate NbS, such as requiring a minimum for green space areas on and around new buildings and permeable material in driveways to increase water absorption and retention capacities.

Public procurement is another key regulatory instrument that can facilitate, or hamper, the use of NbS. Procurement for NbS can include specific construction materials or plant species to be integrated into investments that reduce water-related risks. Country practice demonstrates that more can be done to support NbS through procurement measures. One challenge country practitioners seem to face is the difficulty of demonstrating the full range of the costs and benefits of NbS, which makes it difficult for procurement agencies to follow value-for-money principles that have guided public tendering.

1.4.1. Fostering the use of nature-based solutions through land-use planning and building codes

Spatial plans (land-use or urban planning) shape the built environment and human activity. They define what is permissible in certain areas and in new developments (e.g. building, infrastructure) and can thereby play a critical role in fostering (or inhibiting) the use of NbS. The UK National Policy Planning Framework specifically encourages local authorities, who are in charge of developing local land-use plans and issuing land-use permits, to maintain and enhance green infrastructure. It requires all plans "to use opportunities provided by new development to reduce the causes and impacts of flooding (where appropriate through the use of natural flood management techniques)" (MHCLG, 2019[42]). Norway requires both counties and municipalities to consider the use of NbS in planning processes before the use of alternatives such as grey infrastructure. If an alternative approach is chosen, authorities must provide the government with justification for their decision (Lovdata, 2018[50]).

Building codes and regulations can also encourage the use of NbS. Some countries and municipalities are setting up NbS-specific regulations, such as requirements for new buildings to be equipped with a green roof or a green space minimum for certain areas (Hawxwell et al., 2019[38]). In 2009, Toronto (Canada) became the first North American city to adopt a Green Roof Bylaw that stipulates that new developments covering more than 2 000 m² require green roofs (City of Toronto, 2021[51]). Copenhagen (Denmark) also mandated in 2010 that green roofs be included for a majority of large buildings (City of Copenhagen, 2015[52]). In the United Kingdom, the 2016 London Plan requires that "major development proposals should be designed to include [...] green roofs and walls where feasible" to deliver adaptation to climate change and sustainable urban drainage benefits (Government of London, 2021[53]). In the absence of prescriptions of NbS in building codes, the local government of Mexico City provides a 10% reduction in property tax for installing green roofs (Mexico Daily Post, 2019[54]). Certification schemes with NbS criteria, notably for vegetation use, such as BREEAM and LEED[4] in the building sector, can also facilitate the use of NbS (UNaLab, 2021[55]).

However, despite emerging good practices, case study interviewees in both Mexico and the United Kingdom noted that regulatory frameworks are complex and result in high resource and transaction costs. It is difficult for practitioners to navigate the many and complex regulations from land-use zoning to permitting and safety and performance codes. This can lead to grey infrastructure solutions being favoured. Both countries are undertaking reviews to understand how such bottlenecks can be better addressed (e.g. forthcoming IMTA study in Mexico and Defra's study *The Enablers and Barriers to the Delivery of Natural Flood Management Projects* in the United Kingdom (Defra, 2020[56])). Defra's study highlights several regulatory bottlenecks, such as complex funding application processes as well as approvals and planning processes and excessive requirements on performance information for funding applications (e.g. modelling). To help address these bottlenecks, Defra suggests identifying ways to maximise the multiple benefits of NbS and creating guidance to help practitioners and local planning authorities navigate regulations that apply to NbS projects (Defra, 2020[56]).

In addition, there are also a number of legal complexities related to NbS in terms of land ownership and liability. Case study interviewees highlighted that landowners, and those leasing land, are often concerned over liability for potential maintenance, damage to land and a loss of control of their land. Those who own or manage the land (e.g. landowners or water companies) are not necessarily those who are in charge of the NbS project (e.g. public/private bodies) and may have technical or financial difficulties to maintain the optimal functioning of NbS. Therefore, it is important to clearly define long-term responsibilities.

1.4.2. Integrating nature-based solutions into procurement processes

Certain requirements can make it difficult for NbS to compete in traditional public procurement procedures. Project proposals need to demonstrate the socio-economic and environmental benefits, which are difficult to quantify for NbS. This information is highly site-specific and depends on the NbS' project features, whereby the maintenance cost structure can vary depending on the development over time or climatic and ecosystem conditions. A lack of experience on NbS among procurement practitioners does not facilitate the use of public procurement for encouraging NbS (European Commission, 2020[57]). Germany created the Competence Centre for Innovative Procurement (KOINNO), an online platform that educates and provides consultation on public procurement with best practices for NbS to advise staff on design and implementation processes for these projects (European Commission, 2020[57]). The Global Commission on Adaptation is developing a training course on public-private partnerships for climate-resilient infrastructure, which includes capacity building for green infrastructure (GCA, 2021[58]). Adapting specific clauses in public tenders can encourage the use of NbS while supporting biodiversity, for example, by requiring the use of specific construction materials or native plant species that can bring environmental, flood or drought management benefits to the management of public buildings or spaces.

1.4.3. Supporting nature-based solutions through specific guidelines and standards

As a complement to regulatory requirements, standards and other guidelines are being developed to increase the quality of NbS interventions. For example, the International Union for the Conservation of Nature developed the first-global standard for NbS to help users design, implement and verify NbS actions. It is intended for governments, business and civil society to provide clear parameters for defining NbS and a common framework to help benchmark progress (IUCN, 2020[59]). In England, Natural England is helping to deliver on a commitment under the 25 Year Environment Plan to develop a practical national green infrastructure standard to help local authorities, developers, landowners and communities to deliver more good quality green infrastructure across England (Natural England, 2020[60]). The Mexican city of Hermosillo, for example, developed technical guidelines, including a *Green Infrastructure Design*

Guidelines Manual for Mexican Municipalities and a technical standard for green infrastructure for industrial, commercial and housing developers (Villa, 2018[61]). By contributing to some form of standardisation, these efforts can help reduce transaction costs.

The EU is working towards the creation of a common classification system for sustainable economic activities to facilitate sustainable investment. As per the EU Taxonomy Regulation (EU 2020/852) and the technical screening criteria, an economic activity that favours NbS over grey measures to address adaptation qualifies as doing no significant harm to adaptation, which is one of the conditions for an economic activity to be environmentally sustainable (EU Technical Expert Group on Sustainable Finance, 2020[62]).

1.5. Strengthening technical capacity

Information is key to identify opportunities for nature-based solutions and trigger action

More information needs to be generated and disseminated on the performance of nature-based solutions (NbS) throughout the projects' life cycle, including their maintenance needs and requirements as well as their effectiveness over time when they are applied at a larger scale. There is also a need for this information regarding hybrid solutions, i.e. NbS implemented as a complement to grey infrastructure. In the absence of this information, uncertainty around an NbS' project performance is often cited as a reason for opting for traditionally engineered solutions.

The novelty and innovation of certain NbS can act as a considerable hurdle for their use. Compiling and communicating increasingly available information on good practices and performance data of NbS, through repositories, guidelines or other design tools, can significantly support the scale at which NbS are used and considered.

1.5.1. Building a solid information base

To successfully design and implement NbS, public and private actors must be aware of their strengths and limitations, as well as have the technical capacity to design and implement them. Having access to NbS project performance data, as well as robust technical and design guidance, helps strengthen technical capacity.

Policy makers and NbS practitioners rely on technical information related to ecosystems to determine and design the NbS measures that are most appropriate for addressing certain risks (IUCN French Commission, 2016[63]). Although estimating natural resource stock is difficult, creating an inventory of existing natural capital and assets provides a basis for estimating the value of services and benefits provided by nature and helps support arguments in favour of NbS (Dasgupta, 2021[64]). The United Kingdom has completed a National Ecosystem Assessment and published guidance on how to apply the natural capital approach[5] in decision making (Defra, 2020[65]).

In addition to information related to ecosystems, there is a need to build on existing information regarding water-related risks in order to effectively identify when and justify why NbS are best suited in a specific area. An increasing number of studies assess the value of the ecosystem services in addressing flood and drought risks in specific areas. Mapping and valuing these can help inform the design of NbS interventions. For example, London's "urban forest", containing over 8.5 million trees, is estimated to provide annual flood mitigation benefits valued at approximately EUR 3 million (Treeconomics, 2015[66]). In addition, a study found that while restoring 100% of the United Kingdom's peatlands would cost between EUR 9 billion and EUR 25 billion, having just 55% of the country's peatland in good status would yield between EUR 51 billion and EUR 58 billion in benefits over a 100-year period (Government of the United Kingdom, 2019[67]). Information about human settlement scenarios and vulnerable groups can also help decision makers better target NbS projects (Hawxwell et al., 2019[38]).

In addition to information on climate risks and ecosystem services, there remains a need to fill information gaps related to the effectiveness of NbS projects to help make their business case and inform decision making. Understanding the longer term climatic changes and projected extremes at a regional scale will also be relevant for supporting decision making. Although monitoring at the project level is critical to gather information about NbS effectiveness, it is rarely integrated from a planning and finance perspective. Certain benefits of NbS can take years, even decades, to be fully realised (e.g. forest regeneration efforts can take a long time before stabilising slopes). To help bridge this gap, monitoring is a requirement for any projects completed through the Defra Natural Flood Management Programme for England. In addition, the EU Valorisation of NbS Projects Initiative found research is still needed on small-scale NbS projects at the urban level and large-scale projects at the catchment level, as well as on individual performance and hybrid solutions with grey infrastructure (European Commission, 2020[46]). The European Commission also notes that more performance information is available on small-scale NbS than on large-scale NbS, such as porous pavements and green roofs. It thereby recommends to develop an up-to-date platform with lessons learnt and implementation costs; it encourages efforts to develop tools that integrate flood risk models, weather prediction models, real-time monitoring systems and smart early-warning systems (European Commission, 2020[68]).

1.5.2. Building capacity with training and tools

Technical competences of NbS practitioners and policy makers for NbS need to be strengthened. Interviewees in the United Kingdom raised the challenge that as NbS are often considered to be a relatively new approach, practitioners are uncertain about their performance and therefore chose solutions whose performance they are more familiar with, such as grey infrastructure. In Mexico, most water sector specialists have traditional engineering backgrounds, while engineering programmes are only slowly starting to incorporate innovative approaches, such as NbS. To help bridge this gap, Mexico has incorporated green infrastructure into an engineering programme hosted by the National Autonomous University of Mexico (Universidad Nacional Autónoma de México, UNAM), where, for example, sand dune conservation is part of the measures taught to prevent coastal erosion.

To help raise awareness and build capacity among policy makers and NbS practitioners, both Mexico and the United Kingdom have started compiling best practices and performance data on the implementation of NbS. The United Kingdom created an evidence directory compiling over 60 case studies highlighting best practices related to natural flood management (Environment Agency, 2017[69]). The EU supports several web platforms to display NbS information, such as Climate ADAPT, Natural Water Retention Measures and the Urban Nature Atlas (European Commission, 2020[46]).

A range of tools, handbooks and technical guidance documents help inform and guide NbS projects. For example, the United Kingdom currently has a range of toolboxes and guidance documents that are available to inform practitioners on the design, implementation and continued management of NbS. In addition, the UK Construction Industry Research and Information Association developed a guidance document for the construction of sustainable urban drainage systems and is preparing a *Natural Flood Management Design Manual*. It aims to support actors designing, specifying and constructing sustainable urban drainage systems to understand and avoid common pitfalls (CIRIA, 2015[70]).

Tools also exist to support decision making. For example, the EU-funded UNaLab developed an NbS technical handbook to guide stakeholders in the selection of NbS most adapted to specific contexts (Eisenberg and Polcher, 2019[71]). In addition, the suite of models known as InVEST (Integrated Valuation of Ecosystem Services and Trade-offs) from Stanford maps and values goods and services from nature and is designed to help decision makers quantify trade-offs and identify natural environments that can most benefit from investment in order to enhance natural capital and deliver ecosystem services for society (Standford University, 2020[72]).

Tools and methods are needed to evaluate many of the benefits of NbS, such as their climate change mitigation or adaptation impact or their contribution to habitat preservation. Benefits left unquantified are overlooked by traditional cost-benefit evaluations and thereby act as a constraint to scaling up their use. The existing methodologies for valuing these effects remain underdeveloped or challenging to apply. Examples of methods and studies that can support decision making include those that assess ecosystem service functions such as through hydraulic assessments; those that assess risk exposure and vulnerability to climate change (e.g. vulnerability assessments); or those that help to deal with risk and uncertainty, such as probability analysis or real option analysis (OECD, 2020[13]) (Dasgupta, 2021[64]) (GIZ, 2017[73]).

1.6. Funding nature-based solutions

Nature-based solutions face a scattered funding landscape

Nature-based solutions (NbS) interventions have distinctive financing needs and standard financing models are not easily adaptable to NbS. Until now, NbS have primarily relied on public funding. This is especially the case for measures that aim to attenuate climate risks for larger areas or communities. In terms of the sources of public funding, the landscape is rather fragmented. NbS are supported by funds dedicated to environmental protection, climate change or disaster risk reduction. Some relevant funds are only gradually making NbS explicitly eligible for funding. In other cases, NbS may be eligible for funding in theory, but the difficulty in demonstrating some of their effects quantitatively (such as ecosystem service enhancement) may give other technical measures the priority.

1.6.1. Diverse sources of public funding are available to support nature-based solutions

Public funding represents the majority of funding for NbS in both Mexico and the United Kingdom. It is supplemented by funding from non-governmental organisations, philanthropies, communities or private companies, such as property developers or water companies. Public funding for NbS emanates from funds for both climate adaptation and mitigation, environmental conservation, water, or those funding measures in disaster risk management. Some projects are also directly funded through urban planning budgets (UNEP, 2021[29]).

Environment and climate change funds are an important source of funding for supporting NbS design and implementation, most often in the form of grants. In Mexico, the National Climate Change Fund, linked to the Biodiversity Endowment Fund, supports NbS for adaptation. Similarly, the UK Nature for Climate Fund allocates over EUR 700 million to plant trees and restore peatland across England (UK 2020 Budget). Disaster risk management funds have increasingly included NbS as eligible measures for funding. The UK Flood and Coastal Resilience Innovation Programme[6] targets resilience actions, including NbS or sustainable urban drainage systems, that increase resilience to flood, coastal or drought risks. The fund specifically excludes grey infrastructure such as walls (Government of the United Kingdom, 2021[74]). Large pools of funding available for grey infrastructure have also started to fund NbS projects, such as Canada's EUR 1.3 billion Disaster Mitigation and Adaptation Fund.[7] The eligibility of NbS is not yet a common practice. In Mexico, the disaster prevention fund (i.e. FOPREDEN), which is a significant pool of funding, excludes NbS, as it is currently not considered as a form of structural prevention. Another key obstacle is the valuation and quantification of some of the benefts of NbS (such as ecosystem service enhancement). While *de facto* eligible for funding, in practice NbS are outperformed by other solutions.

Multilateral development banks, development finance institutions, dedicated funds (such as the Global Environment Facility, the Adaptation Fund or the Green Climate Fund) and bilateral donors also provide an important source of funding for NbS projects worldwide. In Mexico, these have funded projects to reduce climate-related risks in the Gulf of Mexico.

A challenge that practitioners face is accessing funding over the NbS' project life cycle. Similar to grey infrastructure, NbS projects require funding over time for maintaining the project's performance. For instance, resources might be needed to ensure slope restabilisation, pest monitoring or invasive species removal in some types of NbS. However, case study interviewees noted that these resource needs are often not factored into initial budgets for NbS projects. For example, in Mexico, most conservation-based programmes are subject to annual budgets. The lack of funding for continued maintenance can lead project implementers, such as landowners, to be reluctant so as to avoid liabilities for costly long-term maintenance or in the case of an NbS project's failure.

1.6.2. Mobilising private finance

For NbS that are characterised by strong public good features, public funding is important. For NbS that benefit specific private actors, or co-benefit them, private (co-)funding should be mobilised. For this it is important to make the business case for NbS. There are a growing number of successful examples of privately funded NbS projects. For instance, water companies (e.g. Scottish Water, Anglian Water and Severn Trent in the United Kingdom) finance the protection of catchments or the creation of wetlands to improve water quality.

Public sources can be important in mobilising additional private finance. Defra and partners[8] joined forces to provide seed grants to four NbS pilot projects to be supplemented by private funding. The private funds are to be paid back by the potential NbS beneficiaries (e.g. water company, the Environment Agency, local authorities, the insurance industry, local stakeholders) (The Flood Hub, n.d.[75]). At the regional level, the Inter-American Development Bank leveraged an additional USD 55 million for projects with the private sector as part of its Natural Capital Lab for improving land use, agriculture and marine ecosystems (Dasgupta, 2021[64]).

Governments incentivise private actors, such as landowners, farmers and foresters, to implement NbS initiatives on private land through various schemes, such as land stewardships schemes, carbon or biodiversity offsets (e.g. planting woodlands, hedge planting or floodplain restoration). While they might not be implemented with water risk management objectives as such, they help mobilise private investment in schemes that deliver quantifiable and valued services, such as Mexico's Payment for Hydrological Services Program for forest conservation.

Private actors also use proceeds from a range of instruments to fund NbS projects, including those from water tariffs. Some water companies in England and Wales are financing NbS out of tariff revenues. Ofwat, the national economic regulator for water services, agreed to include an outcome-based payment in its tariff-setting formula linked to utilities' environmental performance and specifically authorised these companies to use their revenues for such purposes. Severn Trent, for instance, invested its own resources gathered from water tariffs and mobilised matching funding from other sources (Trémolet et al., 2019[76]).

The insurance industry can play a role in fostering NbS. It can incentivise NbS measures with reduced premiums (e.g. on flood insurance) to customers investing in NbS. For example, the insurance industry played a role in developing the Coastal Zone Management Trust of Quintana Roo (Mexico). Established in 2019, the trust collects hotel and tourism concessions to fund coral reef maintenance activities and to purchase a novel parametric insurance policy for hurricane-induced coral reef damage. If a hurricane exceeding a specific wind speed occurs, the insurance coverage will be used to repair the reef (Bechauf, 2020[77]).

References

Bauduceau, N. et al. (2015), *Towards an EU Research and Innovation Policy Agenda for Nature-based Solutions and Re-naturing Cities: Final Report of the Horizon 2020 Expert Group on 'Nature-based Solutions and Renaturing Cities'*, http://dx.doi.org/10.2777/765301. [12]

Bechauf, R. (2020), *Building the Investment Case for Nature-Based Infrastructure*, International Institute for Sustainable Development, Winnipeg, Manitoba, Canada, https://www.iisd.org/articles/investment-case-for-nature-based-infrastructure. [77]

CBD (2018), *Decision Adopted by the Conference of the Parties to the Convention on Biological Diversity*, Convention on Biological Diversity, https://www.cbd.int/doc/decisions/cop-14/cop-14-dec-05-en.pdf. [16]

Chausson et al. (2020), *Mapping the effectiveness of Nature-based Solutions for climate change adaptation*, Glob Change Biol. 2020, https://doi.org/10.1111/gcb.15310. [6]

CIRIA (2015), *Guidance on the Construction of SuDS*, Construction Industry Research and Information Association, London, https://www.ciria.org/news/CIRIA_news2/CIRIA_publishes_new_guidance_on_SuDS_construction.aspx. [70]

City of Copenhagen (2015), *Green Roofs Copenhagen*, Technical and Environment Administration, City of Copenhagen, Copenhagen, https://www.klimatilpasning.dk/media/631048/green_roofs_copenhagen.pdf. [52]

City of Toronto (2021), "Green roofs", webpage, City Planning Division, City of Toronto, Toronto, Canada, https://www.toronto.ca/city-government/planning-development/official-plan-guidelines/green-roofs. [51]

Coe, S. and J. Finlay (2020), "The Agriculture Act 2020", briefing paper No. CBP 8702, House of Commons Library, https://commonslibrary.parliament.uk/research-briefings/cbp-8702/ (accessed on 22 January 2021). [40]

Cohen-Shacham, E et al. (eds) (2016), *Nature-based solutions to address global societal challenges*, IUCN, http://dx.doi.org/10.2305/iucn.ch.2016.13.en. [11]

Dasgupta, P. (2021), *The Economics of Biodivesity: The Dasgupta Review*, HM Treasury, https://www.gov.uk/government/publications/final-report-the-economics-of-biodiversity-the-dasgupta-review. [64]

Defra (2020), *Enabling a Natural Capital Approach: Guidance*, Department of Environment, Food and Rural Affairs, https://www.gov.uk/guidance/enabling-a-natural-capital-approach-enca. [78]

Defra (2020), *Enabling a Natural Capital Approach: Guidance*, Department of Environment, Food & Rural Affairs, https://www.gov.uk/guidance/enabling-a-natural-capital-approach-enca. [65]

Defra (2020), *The Enablers and Barriers to the Delivery of Natural Flood Management Projects*, Department for Environment, Food & Rural Affairs, London, http://sciencesearch.defra.gov.uk/Document.aspx?Document=14754_FD2713_Final_Report.pdf. [56]

Defra (2011), *Biodiversity 2020: A Strategy for England's Wildlife and Ecosystem Services*, Department for Environment, Food & Rural Affairs, London, https://assets.publishing.service.gov.uk/government/uploads/system/uploads/attachment_data/file/69446/pb13583-biodiversity-strategy-2020-111111.pdf. [23]

EA (2017), *Natural flood management – part of the nation's flood resilience*, Environment Agency, https://www.gov.uk/government/news/natural-flood-management-part-of-the-nations-flood-resilience. [14]

Edwards, P., A. Sutton-Grier and G. Coyle (2013), "Investing in nature: Restoring coastal habitat blue infrastructure and green job creation", *Marine Policy*, Vol. 38, pp. 65-71, http://dx.doi.org/10.1016/j.marpol.2012.05.020. [9]

eftec, Environmental Finance and Countryscape (2019), *Greater Manchester Natural Capital Investment Plan*, Greater Manchester Combined Authority, https://naturegreatermanchester.co.uk/project/greater-manchester-natural-capital-investment-plan. [30]

Eisenberg, B. and V. Polcher (2019), *Nature Based Solutions: Technical Handbook*, University of Stuttgart, Stuttgart, Germany, https://www.researchgate.net/publication/332230725_Nature_Based_Solutions_-_Technical_Handbook. [71]

Environment Agency (2017), *Working with Natural Processes to Reduce Flood Risk: The Evidence Base for Working with Natural Processes to Reduce Flood Risk*, Environment Agency, https://www.gov.uk/government/publications/working-with-natural-processes-to-reduce-flood-risk. [69]

EU (2020), *EU recovery plan and long-term EU budget 2021-2027*, European Union, https://www.consilium.europa.eu/en/infographics/recovery-plan-mff-2021-2027/. [31]

EU Technical Expert Group on Sustainable Finance (2020), *Taxonomy Report: Technical Annex*, European Commission, Brussels, https://ec.europa.eu/info/sites/info/files/business_economy_euro/banking_and_finance/documents/200309-sustainable-finance-teg-final-report-taxonomy-annexes_en.pdf. [62]

European Commission (2021), *Forging a Climate-resilient Europe: The New EU Strategy on Adaptation to Climate Change*, European Commission, Brussels, https://ec.europa.eu/clima/sites/clima/files/adaptation/what/docs/eu_strategy_2021.pdf. [26]

European Commission (2020), *Nature-based Solutions for Flood Mitigation and Coastal Resilience*, Publications Office of the European Union, Luxembourg, https://op.europa.eu/fr/publication-detail/-/publication/d6e80dca-d530-11ea-adf7-01aa75ed71a1/language-en/format-PDF/source-142701485. [68]

European Commission (2020), *Nature-based Solutions: State of the Art in EU-funded Projects*, Publications Office of the European Union, Brussels, http://dx.doi.org/10.2777/236007. [46]

European Commission (2020), *Public Procurement of Nature-based Solutions*, Publications Office of the European Union, Luxembourg, http://dx.doi.org/10.2777/561021. [57]

FAO (2019), "Forests: Nature-based solutions for water", *Unasylva*, Vol. 70, Food and Agriculture Organization of the United Nations, Rome, http://www.fao.org/3/ca6842en/CA6842EN.pdf. [20]

Filoso, S. et al. (2017), "Impacts of forest restoration on water yield: A systematic review", *PLoS ONE*, Vol. 12/8, http://dx.doi.org/10.1371/journal.pone.0183210. [5]

Frantzeskaki, N. (2019), "Seven lessons for planning nature-based solutions in cities", *Environmental Science & Policy*, Vol. 93, pp. 101-111, https://doi.org/10.1016/j.envsci.2018.12.033. [48]

GCA (2021), "GCA and the World Bank Group launch the PPPs for Climate-Resilient Infrastructure Knowledge Module", press release, Global Center on Adaptation, https://gca.org/news/gca-and-the-world-bank-group-launch-the-ppps-for-climate-resilient-infrastructure-knowledge-module. [58]

GIZ (2017), *Valuing Benefits, Costs and Impacts of Ecosystem-based Adaptation Measures: A sourcebook of methods for decision-making*, https://www.adaptationcommunity.net/wp-content/uploads/2017/12/EbA-Valuations-Sb_en_online.pdf. [73]

Government of Chile (2020), *Chile's Nationally Determined Contribution*, https://www4.unfccc.int/sites/ndcstaging/PublishedDocuments/Chile%20First/Chile%27s_NDC_2020_english.pdf. [27]

Government of Colombia (2020), *Con el nuevo 'Compromiso por el Futuro de Colombia', el país está haciendo las grandes apuestas: Duque [With the new 'Commitment to the Future of Colombia', the country is making the big bets: Duque]*, Government of Colombia, https://idm.presidencia.gov.co/prensa/Paginas/Con-el-nuevo-Compromiso-por-el-Futuro-de-Colombia-el-pais-esta-haciendo-las-grandes-apuestas-Duque-200820.aspx. [36]

Government of Finland (2020), *Government reaches agreement on fourth supplementary budget proposal for 2020*, Government Communications Department, Ministry of Finance, https://valtioneuvosto.fi/en/-/10616/hallitus-paatti-vuoden-2020-neljannesta-lisatalousarvioesityksesta. [35]

Government of France (2020), *France Relance*, Government of France, https://www.economie.gouv.fr/files/files/directions_services/plan-de-relance/annexe-fiche-mesures.pdf. [34]

Government of Germany (2020), *Corona-Folgen bekämpfen, Wohlstand sichern, Zukunftsfähigkeit stärken [Fighting the consequences of corona, securing prosperity, strengthening future viability]*, Government of Germany, https://www.bundesfinanzministerium.de/Content/DE/Standardartikel/Themen/Schlaglichter/Konjunkturpaket/2020-06-03-eckpunktepapier.pdf?__blob=publicationFile&v=8. [33]

Government of London (2021), "Policy 5.11 Green roofs and development site environs", webpage, Mayor of London, London, https://www.london.gov.uk/what-we-do/planning/london-plan/past-versions-and-alterations-london-plan/london-plan-2016/london-plan-chapter-five-londons-response/pol-10. [53]

Government of Mexico (2020), *Nationally Determined Contributions: 2020 Update*, National Institute of Ecology and Climate Change, Mexico City, https://www4.unfccc.int/sites/ndcstaging/PublishedDocuments/Mexico%20First/NDC-Eng-Dec30.pdf. [28]

Government of Mexico (2020), *Programa Nacional Hídrico PNH 2020-2024 [National Water Program PNH 2020 2024]*, National Commission on Water, https://www.gob.mx/conagua/documentos/programa-nacional-hidrico-pnh-2020-2024. [37]

Government of Mexico (2020), *Programa Sectorial de Medio Ambiente y Recursos Naturales (Promarnat) 2020-2024 [Sectorial Program for the Environment and Natural Resources (Promarnat) 2020-2024]*, Federal Attorney for Environmental Protection, https://www.gob.mx/profepa/acciones-y-programas/programa-sectorial-de-medio-ambiente-y-recursos-naturales-promarnat-2020-2024. [21]

Government of Mexico (2017), *Estrategia de Cambio Climático desde las Áreas Naturales Protegidas: Una Convocatoria para la Resiliencia de México 2015-2020 [Climate Change Strategy from Natural Protected Areas: A Call for Mexico's Resilience 2015-2020]*, National Commission of Natural Protected Areas, https://www.gob.mx/conanp/documentos/estrategia-de-cambio-climatico-desde-las-areas-naturales-protegidas-una-convocatoria-para-la-resiliencia-de-mexico-2015-2020. [22]

Government of Mexico (2016), *Estrategia Nacional sobre Biodiversidad de México y Plan de Acción 2016-2030 [National Strategy on Biodiversity of Mexico and Action Plan 2016-2030]*, National Commission for the Knowledge and Use of Biodiversity, https://www.biodiversidad.gob.mx/pais/enbiomex. [24]

Government of New Zealand (2020), *$1.1 billion investment to create 11,000 environment jobs in our regions: Media release 14 May 2020*, Office of the Minister of Conservation, the Minister for the Environment and the Minister of Agriculture, https://www.doc.govt.nz/news/media-releases/2020-media-releases/investment-to-create-11000-environment-jobs-in-our-regions/. [32]

Government of the United Kingdom (2021), "Flood and Coastal Resilience Innovation Programme", webpage, Environment Agency, https://www.gov.uk/guidance/flood-and-coastal-resilience-innovation-programme#eligible-actions. [74]

Government of the United Kingdom (2019), *UK Natural Capital: Peatlands*, Office for National Statistics, https://www.ons.gov.uk/economy/environmentalaccounts/bulletins/uknaturalcapitalforpeatlands/naturalcapitalaccounts. [67]

Han, S. and C. Kuhlicke (2019), "Reducing hydro-meteorological risk by nature-based solutions: What do we know about people's perceptions?", *Water*, Vol. 11/12, https://doi.org/10.3390/w11122599. [19]

Hawxwell, T. et al. (2019), *Municipal Governance for Nature-based Solutions: Executive Summary of the UNALAB Municipal Governance Guidelines*, European Regions Research and Innovation Network, https://errin.eu/documents/municipal-governance-nature-based-solutions. [38]

IUCN (2020), *IUCN Global Standard for Nature-based Solutions: A User Friendly Framework for the Verification, Design and Scaling Up of NbS: First Edition*, International Union for Conservation of Nature, https://doi.org/10.2305/IUCN.CH.2020.08.en. [59]

IUCN French Commission (2016), *Nature-based Solutions to Address Climate Change*, IUCN French Commission, Paris, https://uicn.fr/wp-content/uploads/2016/09/Plaquette-Solutions-EN-07.2016.web1_.pdf. [63]

JNCC and Defra (2012), *UK Post-2010 Biodiversity Framework*, Four Countries' Biodiversity Group, Peterborough, England, https://jncc.gov.uk/our-work/uk-post-2010-biodiversity-framework. [25]

Kabisch, N. et al. (2016), "Nature-based solutions to climate change mitigation and adaptation in urban areas: Perspectives on indicators, knowledge gaps, barriers, and opportunities for action", *Ecology and Society*, Vol. 21/2, https://www.jstor.org/stable/26270403. [2]

Lovdata (2018), *State Planning Guidelines for Climate and Energy Planning and Climate Adaptation*, Ministry of Local Government and Modernization, Oslo, https://lovdata.no/dokument/SF/forskrift/2018-09-28-1469. [50]

Masson-Delmotte, V. et al. (eds.) (2018), *Global Warming of 1.5°C*, Intergovernmental Panel on Climate Change, https://www.ipcc.ch/sr15. [1]

Menéndez, P. et al. (2020), "The global flood protection benefits of mangroves", *Scientific Reports*, Vol. 10/1, pp. 1-11, http://dx.doi.org/10.1038/s41598-020-61136-6. [8]

Mexico Daily Post (2019), "The largest green roof in Latin America is in Mexico City", *The Mazatlan Post*, https://themazatlanpost.com/2019/01/20/the-largest-green-roof-in-latin-america-is-in-mexico-city. [54]

MHCLG (2019), *National Planning Policy Framework*, Ministry of Housing, Communities & Local Government, London, https://assets.publishing.service.gov.uk/government/uploads/system/uploads/attachment_data/file/810197/NPPF_Feb_2019_revised.pdf. [42]

Narayan, S. et al. (2016), "The effectiveness, costs and coastal protection benefits of natural and nature-based defences", *PLoS ONE*, Vol. 11/5, http://dx.doi.org/10.1371/journal.pone.0154735. [4]

Natural England (2020), *A Rapid Scoping Review of Health and Wellbeing Evidence for the Framework of Green Infrastructure Standards*, Natural England, http://publications.naturalengland.org.uk/publication/4799558023643136. [60]

OECD (2021), "Strengthening adaptation-mitigation linkages for a low-carbon, climate-resilient future", *OECD Environment Policy Papers*, No. 23, OECD Publishing, Paris, https://doi.org/10.1787/6d79ff6a-en. [44]

OECD (2021), *Thematic meeting of the Task Force on Climate Change Adaptation, held on the Wednesday 3 March 2021*, http://www.oecd.org/env/cc/climate-adaptation/scalingupnature-basedsolutionstoaddresswater-relatedclimaterisksinsightsfromcountryexperiences. [49]

OECD (2021), *Toolkit for Water Policies and Governance: Converging Towards the OECD Council Recommendation on Water,*, OECD Publishing, https://doi.org/10.1787/ed1a7936-en. [18]

OECD (2020), *Agricultural Policy Monitoring and Evaluation 2020*, OECD Publishing, Paris, https://dx.doi.org/10.1787/928181a8-en. [41]

OECD (2020), *Common Ground Between the Paris Agreement and the Sendai Framework: Climate Change Adaptation and Disaster Risk Reduction*, OECD Publishing, Paris, https://doi.org/10.1787/3edc8d09-en. [43]

OECD (2020), "Nature-based solutions for adapting to water-related climate risks", *OECD Environment Policy Papers*, No. 21, OECD Publishing, Paris, https://dx.doi.org/10.1787/2257873d-en.

[13]

OECD (2019), *Biodiversity: Finance and the Economic and Business Case for Action*, OECD Publishing, Paris, https://dx.doi.org/10.1787/a3147942-en.

[10]

RSPB (2015), *Medmerry Coastal Realignment: Success for People and Wildlife*, Royal Society for the Protection of Birds, https://ww2.rspb.org.uk/Images/medmerry_tcm9-405348.pdf.

[47]

RSPB (n.d.), "Wallasea Island", webpage, Royal Society for the Protection of Birds, https://www.rspb.org.uk/reserves-and-events/reserves-a-z/wallasea-island.

[45]

Seddon, N. et al. (2019), *Synthesis and Recommendations for Enhancing Climate Ambition and Action by 2020 Nature-based Solutions in Nationally Determined Contributions*, International Union for Conservation of Nature, http://portals.iucn.org/library/node/48525.

[17]

Standford University (2020), "InVEST: Natural Capital Project", webpage, Standford University, https://naturalcapitalproject.stanford.edu/software/invest.

[72]

The Flood Hub (n.d.), "Wyre NFM Project", webpage, The Flood Hub, http://thefloodhub.co.uk/wyre-nfm-project.

[75]

The Nature Conservancy Business Council (2019), *Strategies for Operationalizing Nature-based Solutions in the Private Sector*, The Nature Conservancy, https://www.preventionweb.net/publications/view/66907.

[7]

Treeconomics (2015), *Valuing London's Urban Forest: Results of the London i-Tree Eco Project*, Treeconomics, London, https://www.forestresearch.gov.uk/documents/7885/London-i-Tree-Report.pdf.

[66]

Trémolet, S. et al. (2019), *Investing in Nature for European Water Security*, The Nature Conservancy, Ecologic Institute and ICLEI, London, https://www.nature.org/content/dam/tnc/nature/en/documents/Investing_in_Nature_for_European_Water_Security_02.pdf.

[76]

UNaLab (2021), "G16 encouraging the use of certification schemes and sustainability programs", Urban Nature Lab, https://unalab.eu/en/node/160.

[55]

Underwoord, E. and G. Tucker (2016), *Ecological Focus Areas: What Are Their Impacts on Biodiversity?*, Institute for European Environmental Policy, https://ieep.eu/publications/ecological-focus-areas-what-impacts-on-biodiversity.

[39]

UNEP (2021), *Adaptation Gap Report 2020*, United Nations Environment Programme, Nairobi, http://www.unenvironment.org/resources/adaptation-gap-report-2020.

[29]

UNFCCC (2020), *Report of the Conference of the Parties on its Twenty-fifth Session, Held in Madrid from 2 to 15 December 2019*, United Nations Framework Convention on Climate Change, https://unfccc.int/sites/default/files/resource/cp2019_13a01E.pdf.

[15]

van der Geest, K. et al. (2019), "The impacts of climate change on ecosystem services and resulting losses and damages to people and society", in Mechler, R. et al. (eds.), *Loss and Damage from Climate Change: Concepts, Methods and Policy Options*, Springer, Cham, http://dx.doi.org/10.1007/978-3-319-72026-5_9.

[3]

Villa, A. (2018), *Green Infrastructure in Mexico: A Booster for Healthier Cities*, Urbanet, http://www.urbanet.info/mexico-green-infrastructure.

[61]

Annex 1.A. Questionnaire

ACTORS AND INSTITUTIONAL ARRANGEMENTS

1. Who are the key government authorities with a mandate to undertake **planning** for the management of water-related risks? This includes assessing areas at risk of flooding (riverine, coastal, urban) and drought, and prioritising different interventions to manage these risks. *Please fill in the table below with the authority's name and role, and both national and subnational levels, if applicable. Please add rows if needed.*

    a. Of the stakeholders listed in the table below, in the column on the right, please rank the level of awareness of NbS on a scale of 1-5 with 1 being low and 5 being high.

Table i: Planning

Authority name	Role	Awareness of NbS, on a scale of 1-5

2. Who are the key government authorities who **implement** measures to manage water-related risks? This includes engaging stakeholders, securing financing, and overseeing construction and maintenance. *Please fill in the table below with the authority's name and role, and both national and subnational levels, if applicable. Please add rows if needed.*

    a. Of the stakeholders listed in the table below, please rank the level of awareness of NbS on a scale of 1-5 with 1 being low and 5 being high.

Table ii: Implementing

Authority name	Role	Awareness of NbS, on a scale of 1-5

3. Are any private actors involved in the **implementation** of NbS, and if so, what is their role? *Please check those that apply*:

- Landowners (including farmers, forest managers)
- Property developers
- Insurers
- Water utilities
- Other (please specify)

4. Are any private actors involved in the **financing** of NbS, and if so, what types of actors? *Please check those that apply*:

- Landowners (including farmers, forest managers)
- Property developers
- Insurers
- Water utilities
- Other (please specify)

5. Overall, would you say the use of NbS is promoted by the relevant national authorities?
- Yes
- No
- It depends. Please provide more detail.

6. Are there any institutional or governance issues (for example, co-ordination or communication challenges between different departments, levels of government or communities) which have impeded the use of NbS? Please describe.

7. In your opinion, do existing institutional arrangements facilitate the use of NbS? Please explain.

STRATEGIC DIRECTION (POLICIES)

8. Are NbS cited in key national plans/strategies? Please check all that apply, and fill in the name and year of the plan.
- For Mexico: National Development Plan (Name and year)
- National Adaptation Plan (Name and year)
- National Biodiversity Plan
- Disaster Risk Management Plan
- National Infrastructure Delivery Plan (for Mexico: National Infrastructure Investment Plan)
- Other (please list)

9. In those strategies, which sectors have been identified as the most relevant for the use of NbS for managing water-related risks?
- Water management
- Flood risk management
- Agriculture
- Urban development
- Forestry
- Transport
- Other (please list)

10. In your opinion, what have priorities related to NbS been influenced and determined by? (This could include local demand, international policy frameworks, increasing flood risk with climate change, etc.).

11. Have trade-offs between policy objectives related to NbS emerged? (For example, conflict between different land uses or sectoral needs.) If yes, please explain.

12. For the United Kingdom: Have any policies been particularly instrumental in facilitating the use of NbS? If yes, please describe.

LAWS AND REGULATIONS

13. Do any of the following codes, laws or regulations make reference to NbS?
- Local land-use plans
- National building code guidelines
- Local building codes
- Flood safety standards
- Other relevant codes/laws/regulation for the management of water-related risks (please list below)

14. In your opinion, do any of the codes, laws or regulations listed above make the use of NbS challenging? Please explain.

15. In your opinion, do any of the codes, laws or regulations listed above facilitate the use of NbS, and if so, how?

TOOLS AND TECHNICAL CAPACITY

16. Have technical or information gaps related to NbS been identified? *If yes, what are they?*

    a. If yes, are there any measures in place to address these gaps?

    b. In your opinion, are these measures sufficient? If no, any suggestions for improvement?

17. Overall, how would you rank public sector technical capacity with regards to NbS? *Please check below the option that best describes the current situation:*

- High capacity – strong technical knowledge among many related to NbS planning and implementation

- Medium capacity – modest technical knowledge among some related to NbS planning and implementation

- Low capacity – low knowledge among most related to NbS planning and implementation

- Other – please describe

    a. Are there specific areas in government or professions where you think technical capacity is particularly high?

18. Has training to implementing agencies been provided on NbS? *If yes, what has this entailed?*

    a. Has this training been effective? Are there any gaps?

FINANCE

19. What are the main domestic public sources of funding available for protection against risks of floods and droughts? Please check those that apply.

- Subnational funds

- National disaster risk management funds

- Other national funds *(please list)*

- International public funding[9]

- Other *(please list)*

20. Have any of the sources listed above been used to finance NbS? *If yes, please elaborate.*

    a. Do the rules on using any public sources of funding explicitly include NbS? *If yes, please list which ones (e.g. special grants, earmarked funds, etc.).*

    b. In your opinion, could any of the sources listed be used to finance NbS? *If yes, please explain. If no, what do you see as the main bottlenecks?*

21. Are there any other sources of funding that are used to manage water-related risks? Examples include philanthropies, foundations, corporates, other private sector funding.

22. Of the sources listed in Question 19, have any of them been used to fund NbS? *If yes, could you provide an example?*

    a. If no, what do you see as the main bottlenecks?

    b. Is there a rough estimate of the amount the public sector annually invests in NbS?

    c. Is there a rough estimate of the amount the private sector annually invests in NbS?

23. What methodology do you use for considering the costs and benefits of investments (either NbS or grey infrastructure) that reduce exposure to water-related risks? Please specify:

    a. Which categories of costs are included: CAPEX (cost of capital investments), OPEX (cost of operations) or TOTEX (total costs)?

    b. What would be the typical time horizon of financing decisions?

    c. How are co-benefits valued and factored in?

    d. Is flexibility and capacity to adapt to shifting conditions given value? If so, how?

24. In your opinion, do any of the methods listed above support or hinder consideration for NbS? Please develop your answer.

25. Have any *ex ante* assessments of the costs and benefits of NbS compared to grey infrastructure been performed? If so, what have been the results? *(Please fill in the box, or link relevant document).*

26. For Mexico: Who is accountable or liable in case of damage/asset failure? Please check all that apply.

- Asset owner
- Government authority
- Other

GENERAL

27. Are there examples of what you would consider the successful application of NbS in your country? If yes, please describe both the application itself and how you define success.

    a. In your opinion, why was the above project(s) a success?

    b. How was the above project(s) funded?

28. What do you see as the most important opportunities and challenges for the use of NbS to manage water-related risks in your country?

Notes

[1] For more information about the OECD Survey on the Implementation of the Recommendation of the Council on Water, carried out between October 2019 and February 2020, with responses from 26 OECD countries and Costa Rica, see OECD (2021[18]).

[2] As of January 2021, six OECD member countries (including Mexico and the United Kingdom), as well as the European Union had published their second NDC.

[3] The UK Countryside Stewardship is an agri-environment payment that provides financial incentives for farmers, woodland owners, foresters and land managers to look after and improve the environment.

[4] https://www.breeam.com and http://leed.usgbc.org.

[5] The natural capital approach is defined as being a form of policy and decision making that takes into consideration the value of the environment and its services in relation to society and the economy (Defra, 2020[78]).

[6] This programme (GBP 200 million fund) aims to encourage local authorities, businesses and communities to demonstrate innovative practical resilience actions in their areas. Eligible resilience actions include NbS and sustainable drainage systems. Further information is available at: www.gov.uk/guidance/flood-and-coastal-resilience-innovation-programme.

[7] Eligible projects under the Disaster Mitigation and Adaptation Fund include new construction of public infrastructure including natural infrastructure and modification and/or reinforcement, including rehabilitation and expansion of existing public infrastructure including natural infrastructure. Further information is available at: www.infrastructure.gc.ca/dmaf-faac.

[8] Defra, the Environment Agency, Esmée Fairbairn Foundation and Triodos Bank UK.

[9] EU Cohesion Funds, others.

2. Managing water-related climate risks with nature-based solutions in Mexico

This chapter presents the findings of a case study carried out in Mexico on scaling up the use of nature-based solutions to address water-related climate risks. Building on the initial policy framework developed, it presents insights into Mexico's enabling environment for nature-based solutions, specifically with regard to policy, governance and regulatory frameworks, as well as technical capacity and funding for nature-based solutions. It presents challenges Mexico is confronted with as well as evolving good practices to address them.

2.1. Introduction

2.1.1. Context and objective of the case study

Healthy ecosystems and their associated services can provide effective protection against climate-related variability and change, including extreme weather events. Nature-based solutions (NbS)[1] have recently gained momentum as measures that *protect, sustainably manage and restore nature, with the goal of preserving and enhancing ecosystem services to help address societal goals.* For example, restoring a wetland can enhance its water storage capacity, thereby reducing flood risk in neighbouring communities, contributing to better water quality and enhancing species' habitats. NbS can be used as an alternative or complement to service provision through engineered, grey infrastructure, such as by using green roofs or constructed wetlands to prevent drainage systems from being overwhelmed by surface run-off (Depietri and McPhearson, 2017[1]). NbS tend to perform well across a wide range of conditions, and provide diverse benefits, making them particularly well-suited for adapting to a changing and uncertain climate (OECD, 2020[2]).

Recent OECD work on NbS has shown that despite their benefits in managing water-related climate risks, a number of bottlenecks, notably related to governance, regulations, policies and financing, hinder their uptake (OECD, 2020[2]). This paper is one of a series of country case studies that explore existing challenges and aim to identify potential ways to overcome them. This case study provides an overview of the actors and institutions, policies, regulations, technical capacity, and financing which make up the enabling environment for water-related climate risk management in Mexico. It is intended to share best practices and support policy makers in OECD countries in levelling the playing field for NbS. The series of case studies explore the following questions:

- How are NbS mainstreamed into planning and investment decisions for managing water-related climate risks?
- What tools and mechanisms are used to promote NbS?

2.1.2. Overview: Water-related climate risks

Mexico has a diverse natural landscape composed of many different types of ecosystems, ranging from deserts to mountains, lagoons, mangroves and forests (Government of Mexico, 2020[3]). It is widely recognised as being a mega biodiverse country, hosting between 10% and 12% of the world's species (OECD, 2013[4]). Mexico's rich nature has high value to its people and economy. For example, The Nature Conservancy estimates that mangroves protect 300 000 people from flooding and prevent USD 9 billion of property damage from floods annually in Mexico (Losada et al., 2018[5]). In Mexico's Gulf of California and Baja California Peninsula, marine ecosystems support tourism activities. Each year, nature-based marine tourism in the area generates approximately USD 518 million in revenues and around 3 500 directly created jobs (Cisneros-Montemayor et al., 2020[6]). Furthermore, a study on the economic valuation of ecosystem services found that regulation services, which include erosion and flood control, are among the most valuable types of ecosystem services (INECC, 2020[7]). Beyond its abundant natural wealth, Mexico has a high amount of cultural wealth, which is closely linked to ecosystem conservation and the management of natural resources. Historically, the country has had large numbers of cultures settle within its territory, resulting in a diverse population with traditional knowledge regarding environmental conservation and practices (Government of Mexico, 2020[3]).

Due to its location in between the Atlantic and Pacific oceans and its complex topography, Mexico is highly exposed to different water-related hazards, many of which are fuelled or exacerbated by climate change.[2] For example, the country is particularly vulnerable to tropical cyclones, with approximately 40% of the territory being exposed to high or medium tropical cyclone risk. In 2013, Hurricanes Ingrid and Manuel and the resulting heavy rains and landslides caused nearly 200 deaths, affected approximately 155 000 people, and caused around USD 5.7 billion in damages (OECD/The World Bank, 2019[8]). Although floods regularly occur, they are more frequent during the rainy season, between March and November. Furthermore, there is a particularly high risk of landslides and avalanches along Mexico's Sierra Madre mountain range. Close to 300 municipalities are at risk of landslides (INECC, 2019[9]). Finally, Mexico is subject to frequent droughts, resulting in significant agricultural losses. For example, a severe drought heavily affected the region of Guerrero in 2015, ultimately causing around USD 26 million in total economic damages (OECD/The World Bank, 2019[8]).

A growing population and an increase in urbanisation have increased the country's exposure to water-related climate risks. Mexico has a population of approximately 126 million people, with almost 80% of the population living in urban areas (UN DESA, 2018[10]). Approximately 200 cities with a population of more than 10 000 inhabitants are located in river basins with high flood risk (OECD, 2013[11]). Furthermore, many urban populations live in informal settlements that include limited access to services (e.g. emergency services) and housing (USAID, 2017[12]), thus contributing to the vulnerability to water-related risks. Indigenous populations, which compose 21.5% of the country's population, are particularly vulnerable to the impacts of water-related risks, with up to of 70% of these communities living in poverty in 2016 (Roldan, 2018[13]; CDI, 2015[14]).

Climate change is expected to increase the frequency and magnitude of the impacts of water-related climate risks in Mexico. Precipitation is projected to decrease between 10% and 20% in most of the country, while north-western Mexico might experience an increase in precipitation of up to 40% (SEMARNAT and INECC, 2018[15]). A decrease in average rainfall will likely impact the availability of freshwater supplies, while an increase in average rainfall could affect the severity and frequency of flooding. Additionally, with over 11 000 kilometres of coastline, and with about 66% of coasts already dealing with some level of erosion, climate change will exacerbate risks for coastal communities subject to the effects of coastal erosion and storms and flooding due to sea level rise (Score, 2020[16]; Valderrama-Landeros et al., 2019[17]).

Land degradation is also driving vulnerability and exposure to water-related climate risks. Land-use conversion, plant pests and diseases, and overgrazing have degraded land over the past 25 years (CONAFOR, 2015[18]). Conversion of natural landscapes to agricultural and urbanised land has been identified as one of the primary drivers that leads to an increase in the frequency of floods in Mexico, particularly in the south-central region of the country (Zúñiga and Magaña, 2018[19]). Factors such as urbanisation and deforestation result in the deterioration of watersheds, consequently making them more vulnerable to heavy rains and flooding. At present, 50% of Mexico's total land area shows some degree of deterioration, a factor that has made the country increasingly more vulnerable to water-related climate risks (Martínez-Garza, Ceccon and Guariguata, 2018[20]).

2.2. The enabling environment for managing water-related climate risks with nature-based solutions

2.2.1. Actors and institutional arrangements

Many institutions and actors at the national and subnational level play a role in the use of NbS for managing water-related climate risks. Their responsibilities encompass flood and drought management, environmental conservation but also urban planning and broader land-use management, as well as those in charge of environmental preservation measures. Figure 2.1 provides an overview of the national and subnational authorities responsible for implementing NbS to manage water-related climate risks.

Figure 2.1. Overview of the authorities responsible for implementing nature-based solutions to manage water-related climate risks in Mexico

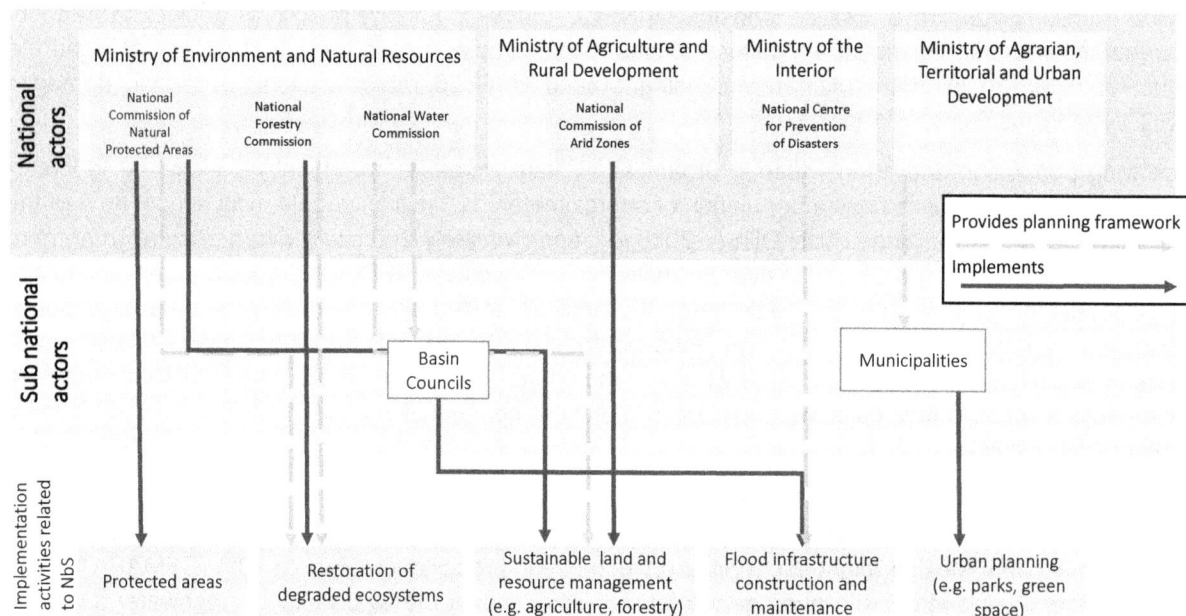

Note: NbS: nature-based solution.

The Ministry of Environment and Natural Resources (Secretaría de Medio Ambiente y Recursos Naturales, SEMARNAT) is the federal authority with the most direct competencies for planning and implementing NbS for managing climate-related water risks. Together with its three decentralised public bodies, these authorities have responsibilities for conservation, restoration, land management and water management:

- The National Commission of Natural Protected Areas (Comisión Nacional de Áreas Naturales Protegidas, CONANP) is responsible for creating and managing protected natural areas, such as national parks, biosphere reserves, sanctuaries or protected areas of flora and fauna. In recent years, this authority has started to incorporate climate change adaptation and disaster risk reduction into its work and to explore how protected areas can be a form of NbS, by leveraging ecosystem services that protected areas provide to the broader landscape. For example, CONANP undertook ecosystem valuation assessments of both sand dunes and coral reefs as a pilot project with the tourism sector.

- The National Forestry Commission (Comisión Nacional Forestal, CONAFOR) is responsible for facilitating sustainable forestry development. While it doesn't have any explicit policies or programmes that consider forest restoration as an NbS, CONAFOR is responsible for forest restoration projects in watersheds, which can address both flooding and drought risk.

- The National Water Commission (Comisión Nacional del Agua, CONAGUA) is responsible for water management, planning and implementation at the national level. Its responsibilities cover flood control infrastructure development, with a focus on major grey investments, as well as a large hydraulic infrastructure network of about 4 000 dams producing electricity, supplying drinking water and regulating water flows (OECD, 2013[11]).

SEMARNAT is also responsible for climate change policy. Its scientific institute, the National Institute of Ecology and Climate Change (Instituto Nacional de Ecología y Cambio Climático, INECC) contributes to the development, conducts and evaluates national policy, and supports capacity building, including on climate change adaptation. INECC works with international donors on climate-related projects, including on NbS pilots. Furthermore, INECC developed action plans for integrated watershed management (*planes de acción para el manejo integral de cuencas hídricas*) that promote integrated management of coastal watersheds to preserve biodiversity and contribute to climate change adaptation and mitigation. Additionally, INECC developed the National Atlas of Vulnerability to Climate Change that includes recommendations for floods, landslides and water stress that encompass the conservation of natural vegetation in basins, payment for ecosystem services and the creation of natural protected areas (INECC, 2019[9]).

The Mexican Institute of Water Technology (Instituto Mexicano de Tecnología del Agua, IMTA) is a decentralised public body of SEMARNAT. It is a public research centre focused on technology development and research on water resources protection, including NbS for water management.

National actors working on environmental issues are considered to have a high level of awareness of NbS and have made efforts to promote their use. However, there are some actors and institutions with key responsibilities for influencing the use of NbS which tend to have a lower awareness of NbS, of their ability to provide multiple functions, as well as of their potential economic benefits. Institutions with great potential to influence the use of NbS include:

- The Ministry of Agriculture and Rural Development (Secretaría de Agricultura y Desarrollo Rural, SADER) is responsible for planning and implementing support programmes for the agricultural sector to help adapt to the effects of severe droughts. NbS present a major opportunity within the agricultural sector in Mexico as they can be used for groundwater recharge, which can then support farms. There are several examples of this having already been implemented, such as in the reforestation that was done in the Izta-Popo National Park (Sonneveld, Merbis and Arnal, 2018[21]). Within SADER, the National Commission of Arid Zones (Comisión Nacional de las Zonas Aridas, CONAZA) has a mandate to manage droughts, as well as rainwater capture. SADER's regional offices provide an opportunity to work directly with local stakeholders as well as to transmit local information back to central authorities.

- The Ministry of the Interior (Secretaría de Gobernación, SEGOB) holds a potentially important role in the use of NbS to reduce exposure to hazards, as its National Centre for Prevention of Disasters (Centro Nacional de Prevención de Desastres, CENAPRED) is responsible for planning for disasters. CENAPRED conducts research and training on the causes of, and how to mitigate the consequences of, disasters. Decision makers use the information collected and recommendations made by CENAPRED to take actions for the prevention of disasters. This provides CENAPRED with a unique opportunity to influence how risks are managed, and for the role of NbS.

- The Ministry of Agrarian, Territorial and Urban Development (Secretaría de Desarrollo Agrario,Territorial y Urbano, SEDATU) is responsible for policies pertaining to urban planning, land use and land tenure. It regulates settlements of both urban and rural communities, land and water related to agriculture, and government strategies for infrastructure. As land use is a critical component of NbS, SEDATU has the opportunity to consider these approaches when going forward with infrastructure projects.

- The National Institute of Indigenous Peoples (Instituto Nacional de los Pueblos Indígenas, INPI) is responsible for recognising, protecting, defending and conserving the lands, territories, assets and natural resources of indigenous peoples. In addition, it promotes and implements measures in co-ordination with indigenous and Afromexican peoples for the conservation and protection of biodiversity and the environment in order to maintain sustainable lifestyles that are resilient to the adverse consequences of climate change.

Given the multi-faceted character of NbS, their uptake could benefit from effective institutional co-ordination and collaboration. There are examples where ministries with different mandates have collaborated on an NbS project. In a project implemented by WWF-Mexico, CONAGUA and CONANP collaborated to ensure that mangrove conservation projects happen in tandem with watershed restoration.

This collaboration is key, as mangroves restoration efforts are much more likely to be successful in healthy watersheds (Barrios Ordóñez, 2015[22]). However, despite overall efforts to collaborate, interviewees recognised that much more could be done to highlight ecosystem interdependencies and systematically bring forward projects with co-benefits across sectors.

In Mexico's federal system, regional and municipal authorities are responsible for land use; construction and zoning permits; housing and ecological preservation; as well as for the creation, evaluation and enforcement of urban development plans (OECD, 2013[11]). This mandate provides municipalities with a potentially important role for promoting the use of NbS. For example, the city of Xalapa introduced rainwater harvesting systems in public buildings and schools to ensure adequate water supplies against unpredictable rainfall (GEF, 2019[23]). In Mexico City, the local government grants a 10% reduction in property tax to incentivise the installation of green roofs to manage storm water runoff and generate other benefits (such as mitigating the urban heat island effect) (Mexico Daily Post, 2019[24]). There is scope for national actors to more systematically monitor and bring forth local level initiatives to promote the uptake of such good practices among subnational peers.

Non-governmental actors, such as landowners (e.g. farmers and forest managers), water utilities, property developers, or sectors with explicit interest in the environment (such as tourism) and insurers can make important contributions to the use of NbS. For example, the car manufacturer Volkswagen de México partnered with CONANP in Puebla-Tlaxcala valley to replant nearby deforested volcanic slopes to improve groundwater replenishment in the valley and build resilience against drought in the region. Increased water supply benefited both the nearby city of Puebla, as well as the operations of the Volkswagen plant (WBCSD, 2018[25]). The tourism sector has also been involved in the deployment of NbS, given the clear business value of protecting coasts and infrastructure from extreme weather events. The national government is working to find more ways to encourage private sector involvement and investment in NbS. A notable ongoing initiative to encourage their involvement is the issuance of green certificates for tourism operators that implement measures to protect the coast, such as dune restoration for the purpose of erosion prevention.

Landowners, including farmers, forest managers and indigenous peoples, are key non-governmental actors. With the Program for the Economic Enhancement of Indigenous Peoples and Communities (Programa para el Fortalecimiento Económico de los Pueblos y Comunidades Indígenas, PROECI), INCI supports conservation strategies and the sustainable management of natural resources by indigenous communities. This programme enabled the implementation of an NbS project of construction and rehabilitation of rainwater catchment works in Oaxaca.

Environmental non-governmental organisations (NGOs), which collaborate with relevant stakeholders and provide local knowledge for NbS projects, are key non-governmental actors. Almost all NbS pilots in Mexico thus far have had NGO involvement. One example of this is the support NGOs provided the city of Merida in accomplishing goals in its Green Infrastructure Plan, specifically through collaborating with the city's tree-planting programme. The plan includes additional projects such as the creation of water bioretention areas, runoff management, and storm water containment in urban parks and roads (The Yucatan Times, 2017[26]).

2.2.2. Policies and regulatory frameworks

Policies, strategies and plans

Table 2.1 illustrates the inclusion of NbS in some of Mexico's key policy documents guiding the country's general, but also sectoral, development (such as in water or climate change). Mexico has traditionally relied on grey infrastructure to manage water-related risks. The incorporation of NbS as a core concept in policies such as the National Water Program (Programa Nacional Hídrico, PNH), the Sector Program for the Environment and Natural Resources (2020-2024) (Programa Sectorial de Medio Ambiente y Recursos

Naturales, Promarnat) represents a fundamental shift in the way both risks and management responses are conceived.

Table 2.1. Selected national bills and policies with relevance to nature-based solutions in Mexico

Name of policy or plan (year)	Purpose	Explicit mention of NbS	Actions related to NbS
National Development Plan (PND) (2019-24)	An overarching strategy document for the federal government with general objectives for the economic and social development of the country.	x	x
National Water Programme (PNH) (2020-24)	Sets the framework for all water management investments in the country, including sustainable water management, increased access to water, increased technical capacities, and increased water security for floods and droughts.	✓	✓
National Strategy on Climate Change (ENCC) (2020-26)*	Sets the strategic direction for climate change adaptation and mitigation policy, including targets to reduce societal vulnerability to water-related climate impacts.	✓	✓
National Biodiversity Strategy and Action Plan (ENBioMex) (2016-20)	Focuses on how to conserve, restore and sustainably manage biodiversity and the services it provides in the short, medium and long term.	x	✓
National General Ecological Spatial Plan* (POEGT) (2020-26)	Aims at regulating land use to protect the environment and to promote sustainable development. It also designates protected areas through the Natural Protected Areas Administration Plan (OECD, 2017[27]).	x	✓
Climate Change Strategy for Protected Areas (ECCAP) (2014-20)	Focuses on increasing the adaptive capacity of ecosystems and the populations that live in them.	✓	✓
National Infrastructure Plan (PNI) (2019-24)	Covers infrastructure planning for six different sectors: energy, tourism, health, urban development, water, and communications and transport.	x	x
National Tourism Strategy (2019-24)*	Contains strategies to diversify the country's tourism sector, reconcile economic growth with social growth and use tourism as a tool to help lift part of the population out of poverty.	x	x
Sector Program for Environment and Natural Resources (Promarnat) (2020-24)	Outlines the environmental policy of the country's current administration, with a focus on topics such as water, food, conservation, energy and education.	✓	✓

Notes: NbS: nature-based solutions. Bills and policies marked with an asterisk are forthcoming.
✓ = yes, x = no.
Sources: Government of Mexico (2019[28]); CONAGUA (2020[29]); CONABIO (2020[30]); SEMARNAT (2016[31]; 2020[32]); CONANP (2017[33]); Fedowitz (2020[34]); Oxford Business Group (2019[35]).

Despite the recognition of NbS in major policy documents, the suggested actions are not underpinned with budgets or implementation responsibilities. For example, in the PNH (2020-2024), the promotion of natural rainwater drainage and restoration measures in high-priority watersheds for building resilience to floods and droughts is highlighted as an action, but information regarding implementation, funding and monitoring is lacking (CONAGUA, 2020[29]). Furthermore, the term NbS is often not specifically mentioned in sectoral policies where NbS could potentially play a key role, such as policies related to infrastructure. Nonetheless, some strategies and plans, such as the Sectoral Program for Tourism 2020-2024 (Programa Sectoral de Turismo, PROSECTUR), emphasise the importance of conserving and restoring ecosystems for adapting to climate change, actions that are considered to be a form of NbS.

While strategic national policies in Mexico are set on a six-year cycle and hence subject to changing priorities, enshrining these policies into law is seen as a way to ensure long-term continuity of objectives, which is essential for NbS. For example, the updated General Law for Water presents an opportunity to put that in practice. While it is not certain whether NbS will be mentioned in the final draft,[3] incorporating an emphasis on natural approaches to water management in this document is a significant opportunity to promote widespread use of NbS.

An ongoing policy challenge is the misalignment of objectives within strategies, which can at times discourage the use of NbS. For example, conservation polices such as the National Biodiversity Action Plan (2016-30) aim to promote the connectivity, conservation and sustainable use of ecosystems. But there are also agricultural and food security objectives that promote an increase in productivity and production goals which often lead to the expansion of agricultural land and can be at odds with the ambition of conservation policies (Cotler and Martínez-Trinidad, 2010[36]; Ojeda, 2017[37]).

Finally, international commitments can play an important role in driving domestic policy. Mexico's first nationally determined contribution under the United Nations Framework Convention on Climate Change (2016) directly refers to NbS such as reforestation and the restoration of ecosystems, bringing prominence to these approaches. Box 2.1 provides an overview of relevant international commitments that Mexico has made in relation to NbS.

Box 2.1. Mexico's international objectives and progress relevant to nature-based solutions for water-related climate risks

Mexico has committed and set objectives that are relevant to nature-based solutions (NbS) through several international frameworks and agreements, demonstrating high-level awareness and commitment to the issue. These include:

- Mexico's 2015 nationally determined contribution submitted under the United Nations Framework Convention on Climate Change includes specific commitments on ecosystem-based adaptation, such as reaching a rate of 0% deforestation by the year 2030. Mexico emphasises the use of NbS for managing water-related risks, with actions listed including the protection, conservation and restoration of watersheds in its updated nationally determined contribution.

- Through the Aichi Target 15 of the Convention on Biological Diversity, Mexico has committed to restoring 15% of its degraded ecosystems, thereby contributing to climate change mitigation and adaptation and to combating desertification.

- Through the Bonn Challenge, Mexico pledged to restore 8.5 million hectares of degraded and deforested landscapes by 2020.

- Through the 2030 Agenda for Sustainable Development, Mexico's Voluntary National Review (2018) includes the country's progress in wetland conservation to meet water-related (SDG 6) goals.

Sources: Government of Mexico (2015[38]; 2018[39]); Ortega-Rubio, (2018[40]); OECD (2018[41]).

Legal and regulatory frameworks

The regulatory framework, which shapes procurement, land-use zones or impact assessments regulations, has an important impact on project level decisions on NbS taken by local governments and non-governmental actors. According to stakeholders that were interviewed (see Annex 2.A.), regulations applying to flood defence infrastructure have been found to be complex and at times to discourage the use of NbS in Mexico.

In order to identify regulatory bottlenecks to the use of NbS, the Mexican Institute of Water Technology initiated research in 2020 to evaluate the regulatory framework for water infrastructure at all levels of government. While the IMTA review is ongoing, examples of potential regulatory obstacles for NbS are emerging:

- National building code guidelines (and most local building codes) do not include NbS as an approach for surface water and run-off management.

- NbS are not considered as a risk reduction measure in disaster models, which are then used to understand vulnerabilities and plan risk reduction investments.

Case study interviewees flagged that hazard insurance policies do not consider NbS as an option to manage risks. For example, many hazard insurance policies require coastal tourism operators, such as hotels, to have a cement wall as storm surge and erosion protection in order to be insurable. However, this fully excludes the use of options that fall under the umbrella of NbS, such as gardens, dunes or vegetation.

There are many opportunities to overcome these regulatory challenges. First, a regulatory review, such as the one IMTA is undertaking, can be a critical first step in both understanding the implementation failures at the local (municipal) level and normative gaps and raising awareness of the issue. Second, the use of guidelines and manuals geared towards actors involved in the planning and implementing stages, such as hydraulic engineers, can be effective in navigating regulatory challenges. The city of Hermosillo, for example, has developed several technical guidelines, including a *Green Infrastructure Design Guidelines Manual for Mexican Municipalities* and a technical standard for green infrastructure that all industrial, commercial and housing developers are required to comply with (Villa, 2018[42]).

2.2.3. Tools and technical capacity

One challenge in Mexico is the limited data that can be readily used to plan NbS. The performance of NbS is highly site-specific and at times complex to assess, and a wide array of data, local information and methodologies may be needed to conduct technical feasibility assessments. While platforms for information sharing on water-related risks and ecosystem conservation exist in Mexico, the information is dispersed across multiple agencies' portals and platforms, making it difficult to obtain all of the information needed to plan an NbS project. For example, CONAGUA is responsible for creating flood hazard maps, while CONANP has previously mapped ecosystems within protected areas and completed ecosystem valuation assessments for several regions of the country. CENAPRED has yet another separate web application that provides layers of geographic information related to disasters such as floods, erosion and fires. In the National Atlas of Vulnerability to Climate Change, INECC assesses the vulnerability to climate change of human settlements to floods and landslides, of livestock production to floods and water stress, of forage production to water stress (INECC, 2019[9]).

Another key gap identified by stakeholders is the lack of historical performance data available on previously implemented NbS projects, and most notably the lack of information on the costs and benefits of NbS compared to other measures. This is in part due to the generally low level of monitoring of NbS-type projects throughout their duration, resulting in little evidence being collected on the projects' costs and benefits, particularly over the long term once the project has been completed. This can represent a major barrier to implementation, as it further prevents the creation of data. Some methods have nonetheless proven their values over time, such as illustrated by the Chinampas system (Box 2.2).

One additional bottleneck to the implementation of NbS is the lack of specialised education in ecological processes for water risk management. Most individuals working in the water sector in Mexico have engineering backgrounds with a focus on building infrastructure that can resist disasters. To increase collaboration, education regarding NbS needs to be mainstreamed across all sectors, rather than just in those related to the environment. Doing so can help to improve awareness and the ability for actors to effectively work with NbS, potentially leading to an increase in the consideration and uptake of these solutions. In recent years, some initiatives and pilots have begun to address this issue. For example, the Engineering Department of the National Autonomous University of Mexico (Universidad Nacional Autónoma de México, UNAM) is integrating green infrastructure into curricula and post-doctoral research projects, providing graduates with skillsets relevant to NbS projects (Watkins et al., 2019[43]). Courses include the use of sand dune conservation and restoration to prevent coastal erosion.

Box 2.2. The role of traditional knowledge in the implementation of nature-based solutions

The Chinampas system, known as a "Globally Important Agricultural Heritage System", is an agro-hydrological system developed by the Aztecs and nowadays used by farmers in Mexico City. It relies on traditional ecological knowledge and understanding of soil conditions to build resilience against drought, using farming methods such as multiple cropping and the shifting of crops. This is in addition to the "Milpa System" of sustainable food production, recognised by the Food and Agriculture Oganization. Currently, the Intersecretarial Group for Health, Food, Environment and Competitiveness (Grupo Intersecretarial de Salud, Alimentación, Medio Ambiente y Competitividad, GISAMAC) promotes the transformation of the food system, through food production based on the knowledge of indigenous peoples and with agro-ecological practices, to improve soil conditions, water conservation and strengthen resilience to the adverse effects of climate change.

Sources: Robles et al. (2018[44]); FAO (2017[45]).

2.2.4. Funding and finance

Like any other investments to manage water-related climate risks, NbS have the potential to be supported by different funding and financing sources, both private and public. According to stakeholders during interviews (see Annex 2.A. for a list of the stakeholders interviewed), the federal government currently does not have an estimate of how much the public or private sector spends on NbS or similar approaches. However, it is estimated that most projects specifically labelled as NbS have been funded through a combination of international assistance and domestic public funds.

The Ministry of Finance and Public Credit (Secretaría de Hacienda y Crédito Público, SHCP) is responsible for managing and allocating Mexico's federal budget. Given the wide range of interventions which can be considered as an NbS, multiple funds have the potential to be used for NbS-related activities (Table 2.2). However, several challenges around the criteria needed to access public funding exist. For example, disaster prevention funds cannot be used to fund NbS, as NbS are not currently considered as a form of structural prevention.

Table 2.2. Examples of public funding mechanisms and sources available for nature-based solutions in Mexico

Fund name	Description
Disaster Assistance Fund (FONDEN) and Disaster Prevention Fund (FOPREDEN)	They can be used to fund the management of water-related risks. While FONDEN is focused on recovery and reconstruction, its funds can currently be used for infrastructure repairs to comply with the latest building codes, as well as housing relocation (OECD, 2013[46]).
National Climate Change Fund (FCC)	The FCC is an endowment fund that mutually supports the Biodiversity Endowment Fund and uses both private and public financial resources for adaptation and mitigation projects. The FCC can potentially be used to fund infrastructure within natural protected areas as well as the creation of new natural protected areas.
Program for the Protection and Restoration of Ecosystems and Species at Risk (PROREST)	Through the support of technical studies and actions, PROREST promotes both the conservation and restoration of ecosystems within natural protected areas by CONANP. This fund can potentially be used for research pertaining to nature-based solutions initiatives that fall under the umbrella of conservation and restoration.
National System of Public Investment (SNIP)	SNIP's institutional framework is used to help strengthen and guide the process of prioritising, planning and selecting projects and investments. It requires certain prerequisites for investment, including cost-benefit analyses and a mechanism for planning which is investment-oriented. The SNIP Environmental Program is used for the financing of conservation, restoration, biodiversity and pollution remediation projects (BIOFIN, 2017[47]).
Budget of Expenditures of the Federation (PEF)	The PEF is the country's general budget that is funded through taxation. Within the PEF is the Transversal Annex on Climate Change (AT-CC), which is set aside to fund projects related to climate change mitigation and adaptation.
Sectorial Fund for Environmental Research SEMARNAT-CONACYT (FSIA)	Created in 2014, the FSIA is used to fund projects in the environment sector. It is generally used to implement initiatives related to increasing resilience to the effects of climate change, infrastructure and the protection of diversity.
Mixed Funds CONACYT (FOMIX)	FOMIX is one of the two funds that makes up the programme budget for the Regional Promotion of Science, Technology and Innovation. It is composed of contributions from both the national and regional governments, and has previously been used for projects such as ecosystem conservation and biodiversity protection.
National Strategic Programs (PRONACES) of CONACYT	PRONACES of CONACYT is used to fund research efforts for subjects that the government deems of importance, with INECC often co-ordinating many of the projects. Examples of subjects that have previously been researched include the effects of climate change on ecosystems, climate change adaptation and ecosystem restoration.

Note: Following the publication of the "Decree ordering the extinction or termination of public trusts, public mandates and similar" (April 2020), which modifies 18 laws and repeals two more, 109 trust are to be extinguished, including the Disaster Assistance Fund (FONDEN); The National Climate Change Fund (FCC); "Sectorial Fund for Environmental Research SEMARNAT-CONACYT (FSIA)" and Mixed Funds CONACYT (FOMIX). The beneficiaries will continue to receive resources through the allocated federal budget.
Source: INECC (2020[48]).

One challenge that was frequently cited by interviewees was around the timing of budgets. For example, most conservation-based programmes are subject to annual budgets, whereas NbS generally need sustained medium- to long-term funding. Depending on the interventions employed, NbS usually require an influx of capital up front that can support initial NbS implementation such as planting trees, removing invasive species, etc. However, to sustain the benefits of an NbS, ongoing maintenance is needed. Additionally, management and monitoring are often not factored into budgets for NbS projects in Mexico, particularly for after a project's completion. This, coupled with a lack of access to medium- and long-term funding and the short mandates of municipal governments frequently makes it difficult for these projects to be sustainable beyond their completion. One potential way to overcome this barrier would be to make NbS eligible for infrastructure funding, as this type of funding is generally multiannual.

Mexico has a well-established payment for ecosystem services programme for forest conservation, known as the Payment for Hydrological Services Programme (Programa de Pago por Servicios Ambientales Hidrológicos, PSAH) (PROFOR, 2019[49]). Administered by CONAFOR, the programme gives forest communities between USD 10 and USD 40 per hectare per year of land conserved and has helped in cutting 38% less forest than they otherwise would have in areas of high risk of deforestation (Alix-Garcia et al., 2014[50]; CBD, 2019[51]). One of the key benefits of this programme is the hydrological management service provided by intact forests – creating a solid model that could be replicated more broadly in Mexico.

Funding and technical support from development agencies and multilateral banks have been key enablers for NbS initiatives in Mexico. For example, between 2011 and 2016, the Global Environmental Facility supported projects to reduce the risk of climate-related disasters in the Gulf of Mexico through NbS, such as mangrove and riparian reforestation, coral reef restoration, and water flow rehabilitation (World Bank, 2018[52]). However, an ongoing challenge is ensuring the continuity of actions once initial project funding has run its course.

Associating NbS benefits with private values can be difficult, especially as many of the potential co-benefits of NbS are hard to monetise, such as increased resilience, avoided losses and non-monetary benefits. Mexico has experience with private actors funding NbS measures in the case where NbS benefits can be translated into direct returns, such as the tourism industry, which depends on wide pristine beaches. One successful example of the private sector financing an NbS project in Mexico is the insurance policy for the Mesoamerican reef in the state of Quintana Roo (Box 2.3). In addition, some communities and local authorities, such as in the Sierra de Zapalinamé in Coahuila, have agreed to encourage water savings through voluntary financial contributions in water bills, revenues of which are then used for the watershed conservation (Gómez, 2016[53]).

Box 2.3. The Mesoamerican Reef insurance policy to protect the reef

The Mesoamerican reef, in the Caribbean Sea, is known for being the second-largest coral reef in the world. It provides coastal flood protection benefits from tropical storms to the local tourism industry as well as other benefits, such as biodiversity protection. As part of a project delivered by The Nature Conservancy and the state government, beachfront property owners are required to pay a fee into a trust to cover the repair of coral reef crest and restore resilience after storm damage as well as beach nourishment. This insurance policy provides protection benefits for buildings valued at USD 42 million, with USD 20.8 million specifically related to hotel infrastructure, while also providing co-benefits related to biodiversity and eco-tourism. The Nature Conservancy is working to determine whether it can be used for other types of ecosystems, such as coastal wetlands, with projects being pursued in Asia, the United States and the Caribbean.

Sources: Reguero et al. (2019[54]); Beck, Quast and Pfliegner (2019[55]); The Nature Conservatory (2019[56]).

References

Alix-Garcia, J. et al. (2014), "Can environmental cash transfers reduce deforestation and improve social outcomes? A regression discontinuity analysis of Mexico's National Program (2011-2014)", *Policy Research Working Paper*, The World Bank, Washington, DC, http://documents.worldbank.org/curated/en/694951547752004287/Can-Environmental-Cash-Transfers-Reduce-Deforestation-and-Improve-Social-Outcomes-A-Regression-Discontinuity-Analysis-of-Mexico-s-National-Program-2011-2014. [50]

Barrios Ordóñez, J. (2015), *National Water Reserves Program in Mexico: Experiences with Environmental Flows and the Allocation of Water for the Environment*, Inter-American Development Bank, https://publications.iadb.org/publications/english/document/National-Water-Reserves-Program-in-Mexico-Experiences-with-Environmental-Flows-and-the-Allocation-of-Water-for-the-Environment.pdf. [22]

Beck, M., O. Quast and K. Pfliegner (2019), *Ecosystem-based Adaptation and Insurance: Success, Challenges and Opportunities*, InsuResilience Global Partnership, Bonn, Germany, https://www.insuresilience.org/wp-content/uploads/2019/11/Ecosystem-based-Adaptation-and-Insurance.pdf. [55]

BIOFIN (2017), *Mexico*, United Nations Development Programme, https://www.biodiversityfinance.org/mexico. [47]

CBD (2019), "Mexico: Financing for biodiversity", webpage, Secretariat of the Convention on Biological Diversity, https://www.cbd.int/financial/mexico.shtml. [51]

CDI (2015), *Numeralia Indígena 2015 [Indigenous Numeralia 2015]*, National Institute of Indigenous People, http://coespo.qroo.gob.mx/Descargas/doc/14%20POBLACI%C3%93N%20INDIGENA/02-numeralia-indicadores-socioeconomicos-2015.pdf. [14]

Cisneros-Montemayor, A. et al. (2020), "Nature-based marine tourism in the Gulf of California and Baja California Peninsula: Economic benefits and key species", *Natural Resources Forum: Special Issue on Oceans*, Vol. 44/2, http://dx.doi.org/10.1111/1477-8947.12193. [6]

CONABIO (2020), "¿Cuál es el contenido? [What is the content?]", webpage, National Commission for the Knowledge and Use of Biodiversity, https://www.biodiversidad.gob.mx/pais/enbiomex/contenido. [30]

CONAFOR (2015), *Prevention and Control of Desertification and Forest Land Degradation in Mexico*, National Forestry Commission of Mexico, http://www.conafor.gob.mx:8080/documentos/docs/7/6156Ing.%20Jorge%20Rescala%20.pdf. [18]

CONAGUA (2020), *Programa Nacional Hídrico 2020-2024 [National Water Program 2020-2024]*, National Commission on Water, https://www.gob.mx/conagua/articulos/consulta-para-el-del-programa-nacional-hidrico-2019-2024-190499. [29]

CONANP (2017), *Estrategia de Cambio Climático desde las Áreas Naturales Protegidas [Climate Change Strategy for Protected Areas]*, National Commission of Natural Protected Areas, https://www.gob.mx/conanp/documentos/estrategia-de-cambio-climatico-desde-las-areas-naturales-protegidas-una-convocatoria-para-la-resiliencia-de-mexico-2015-2020. [33]

Cotler, H. and S. Martínez-Trinidad (2010), "An assessment of soil erosion costs in Mexico", in [36]
Land Degradation and Desertification: Assessment, Mitigation and Remediation, Springer
Netherlands, http://dx.doi.org/10.1007/978-90-481-8657-0_48.

Depietri, Y. and T. McPhearson (2017), "Integrating the grey, green, and blue in cities: Nature- [1]
based solutions for climate change adaptation and risk reduction", in Kabisch, N. et al. (eds.),
*Nature-based Solutions to Climate Change Adaptation in Urban Areas: Theory and Practice
of Urban Sustainability Transitions*, pp. 91-109, Springer, Cham,
http://dx.doi.org/10.1007/978-3-319-56091-5_6.

FAO (2017), "Chinampa system in Mexico", webpage, Food and Agriculture Organization of the [45]
United Nations, Rome, http://www.fao.org/giahs/giahsaroundtheworld/designated-sites/latin-
america-and-the-caribbean/chinampa-system-mexico/detailed-information/en/.

Fedowitz, M. (2020), "Mexico's Infrastructure Plan 2020-2024", *The National Law Review*, [34]
Vol. XI/78, https://www.natlawreview.com/article/mexico-s-infrastructure-plan-2020-2024.

GEF (2019), "Banking on nature: A Mexican city adapts to climate change", webpage, Global [23]
Environment Facility, https://www.thegef.org/news/banking-nature-mexican-city-adapts-
climate-change.

Gómez, S. (2016), "A 20 años de nuevos hallazgos y nuevos retos: Zona sujeta a conservacion [53]
ecologica Sierra Zapalinamé [20 years of new findings and new challenges: Sierra
Zapalinamé Ecological Conservation Area]", *Bordeando El Monte*, No. 36, Ministry of
Environment and Natural Resources,
https://www.sema.gob.mx/descargas/manuales/Bordeando_36.pdf.

Government of Mexico (2020), "México megadiverso [Megadiverse Mexico]", webpage, National [3]
Commission for the Knowledge and Use of Biodiversity,
https://www.biodiversidad.gob.mx/pais/quees.

Government of Mexico (2019), *Plan Nacional de Desarrollo [The National Development Plan]*, [28]
Government of Mexico, https://lopezobrador.org.mx/wp-content/uploads/2019/05/PLAN-
NACIONAL-DE-DESARROLLO-2019-2024.pdf.

Government of Mexico (2018), *Voluntary National Review for the High-Level Political Forum on* [39]
Sustainable Development: Basis for a Long-Term Sustainable Development Vision in Mexico,
United Nations Development Programme,
https://sustainabledevelopment.un.org/content/documents/20122VOLUNTARY_NATIONAL_
REPORT_060718.pdf.

Government of Mexico (2015), *Intended Nationally Determined Contribution*, United Nations [38]
Framework Convention on Climate Change,
https://www4.unfccc.int/sites/submissions/INDC/Published%20Documents/Mexico/1/MEXICO
%20INDC%2003.30.2015.pdf.

INECC (2020), "Presenta INECC propuestas para mejorar acciones de adaptación al cambio [48]
climático [INECC presents proposals to improve adaptation actions to climate change]", press
release, National Institute of Ecology and Climate Change,
https://www.gob.mx/inecc/prensa/presenta-inecc-propuestas-para-mejorar-acciones-de-
adaptacion-al-cambio-climatico?idiom=es.

INECC (2020), *Revisión y Análisis Sobre Valoración Económica de los Servicios Ecosistémicos de México de 1990 a 2019 [Review and Analysis of the Economic Valuation of Mexico's Ecosystem Services from 1990 to 2019]*, National Institute of Ecology and Climate Change, Mexico City, https://www.gob.mx/cms/uploads/attachment/file/579760/Revisio_n_y_analisis_valoracion.pdf . [7]

INECC (2019), *Atlas Nacional de Vulnerabilidad al Cambio Climático [National Atlas of Vulnerability to Climate Change]*, National Institute of Ecology and Climate Change, https://atlasvulnerabilidad.inecc.gob.mx/page/fichas/ANVCC_LibroDigital.pdf . [9]

Losada, I. et al. (2018), *The Global Value of Mangroves for Risk Reduction*, Technical Report, The Nature Conservancy, Berlin, http://dx.doi.org/10.7291/V9DV1H2S . [5]

Martínez-Garza, C., E. Ceccon and M. Guariguata (2018), *La Restauración de Ecosistemas Terrestres en México: Estado Actual, Necesidades y Oportunidades [The Restoration of Terrestrial Ecosystems in Mexico: Current Status, Needs and Opportunities]*, Center for International Forestry Research, https://www.cifor.org/publications/pdf_files/OccPapers/OP-185.pdf . [20]

Mexico Daily Post (2019), "The largest green roof in Latin America is in Mexico City", *The Mazatlan Post*, https://themazatlanpost.com/2019/01/20/the-largest-green-roof-in-latin-america-is-in-mexico-city . [24]

OECD (2020), "Nature-based solutions for adapting to water-related climate risks", *OECD Environment Policy Papers*, No. 21, OECD Publishing, Paris, https://dx.doi.org/10.1787/2257873d-en . [2]

OECD (2018), *Getting it Right: Strategic Priorities for Mexico*, OECD Publishing, Paris, https://dx.doi.org/10.1787/9789264292062-en . [41]

OECD (2017), *Land-use Planning Systems in the OECD: Country Fact Sheets*, OECD Publishing, Paris, https://dx.doi.org/10.1787/9789264268579-en . [27]

OECD (2013), *Making Water Reform Happen in Mexico*, OECD Studies on Water, OECD Publishing, Paris, https://dx.doi.org/10.1787/9789264187894-en . [11]

OECD (2013), *OECD Environmental Performance Reviews: Mexico 2013*, OECD Environmental Performance Reviews, OECD Publishing, Paris, https://dx.doi.org/10.1787/9789264180109-en . [4]

OECD (2013), *OECD Reviews of Risk Management Policies: Mexico 2013: Review of the Mexican National Civil Protection System*, OECD Reviews of Risk Management Policies, OECD Publishing, Paris, https://dx.doi.org/10.1787/9789264192294-en . [46]

OECD/The World Bank (2019), *Fiscal Resilience to Natural Disasters: Lessons from Country Experiences*, OECD Publishing, Paris, https://dx.doi.org/10.1787/27a4198a-en . [8]

Ojeda, G. (2017), *Mexico's Economic and Agricultural Outlook*, Farmfolio, https://farmfolio.net/articles/mexico-economy-agriculture . [37]

Ortega-Rubio, A. (ed.) (2018), *Mexican Natural Resources Management and Biodiversity Conservation*, Springer International Publishing, Cham, http://dx.doi.org/10.1007/978-3-319-90584-6 . [40]

Oxford Business Group (2019), "Mexican government's tourism strategy aims to promote sustainable and inclusive growth", Oxford Business Group, https://oxfordbusinessgroup.com/analysis/all-aboard-government-tourism-strategy-aims-promote-sustainable-and-inclusive-growth-broader-economy. [35]

PROFOR (2019), "In Mexico, payments for ecosystem services benefit forests and communities", webpage, Program on Forests, https://www.profor.info/content/mexico-payments-ecosystem-services-benefit-forests-and-communities. [49]

Reguero, B. et al. (2019), "The risk reduction benefits of the Mesoamerican Reef in Mexico", *Frontiers in Earth Science*, Vol. 7/125, http://dx.doi.org/10.3389/feart.2019.00125. [54]

Robles, B. et al. (2018), "The Chinampa: An ancient Mexican sub-Irrigation system", *Irrigation and Drainage*, Vol. 68/1, pp. 115-122, http://dx.doi.org/10.1002/ird.2310. [44]

Roldan, M. (2018), "Over 70% of indigenous people in Mexico live in poverty", *El Universal*, https://www.eluniversal.com.mx/english/over-70-indigenous-people-mexico-live-poverty. [13]

Score, A. (2020), *Impacts of Climate Change on the Coastal Zone of Mexico: An Integrated Ecosystem Approach in the Gulf of Mexico to Support Coastal Zone Management Legislation*, Climate Adaptation Knowledge Exchange, https://www.cakex.org/case-studies/impacts-climate-change-coastal-zone-mexico-integrated-ecosystem-approach-gulf-mexico-support-coastal-zone-management-legislation. [16]

SEMARNAT (2020), *Programa Sectorial de Medio Ambiente y Recursos Naturales (Promarnat) 2020-2024 [Sector Program for the Environment and Natural Resources (Promarnat) 2020-2024]*, Ministry of the Environment and Natural Resources, https://www.gob.mx/profepa/acciones-y-programas/programa-sectorial-de-medio-ambiente-y-recursos-naturales-promarnat-2020-2024. [32]

SEMARNAT (2016), *Programa de Ordenamiento Ecológico General del Territorio (POETG) [The National General Ecological Spatial Plan]*, Ministry of the Environment and Natural Resources, https://www.gob.mx/semarnat/acciones-y-programas/programa-de-ordenamiento-ecologico-general-del-territorio-poetg. [31]

SEMARNAT and INECC (2018), *Sexta Comunicación Nacional y Segundo Informe Bienal de Actualización ante la Convención Marco de las Naciones Unidas sobre el Cambio Climático [Sixth National Communication and Second Biennial Update Report to the UNFCCC]*, Ministry of the Environment and Natural Resources, National Institute of Ecology and Climate Change, http://cambioclimatico.gob.mx:8080/xmlui/handle/publicaciones/117. [15]

Sonneveld, B., M. Merbis and M. Arnal (2018), "Observations and key messages on nature-based solutions for agricultural water management and food security", brochure, Food and Agriculture Organization of the United Nations, Rome, http://www.fao.org/3/ca2594en/CA2594EN.pdf. [21]

The Nature Conservancy (2019), *Insuring Nature to Ensure a Resilient Future*, The Nature Conservancy, https://www.nature.org/en-us/what-we-do/our-insights/perspectives/insuring-nature-to-ensure-a-resilient-future. [56]

The Yucatan Times (2017), "Merida looking greener as tree-planting program expands", *The Yucatan Times*, https://www.theyucatantimes.com/2017/06/merida-looks-greener-than-before. [26]

UN DESA (2018), *World Urbanization Prospects*, United Nations Department of Economic and [10]
Social Affairs, New York, https://population.un.org/wup/Country-Profiles.

USAID (2017), *Property Rights and Resource Governance: Mexico*, United States Agency for [12]
International Development, Washington, DC, https://www.land-links.org/wp-
content/uploads/2011/03/USAID_Land_Tenure_Mexico_Profile_Revised-December-
2017.pdf.

Valderrama-Landeros, L. et al. (2019), "Dynamics of coastline changes in Mexico", *Journal of* [17]
Geographical Sciences, Vol. 29/10, pp. 1637-1654, http://dx.doi.org/10.1007/s11442-019-
1679-x.

Villa, A. (2018), *Green Infrastructure in Mexico: A Booster for Healthier Cities*, Urbanet, [42]
https://www.urbanet.info/mexico-green-infrastructure.

Watkins, G. et al. (2019), *Nature-based Solutions: Scaling Private Sector Uptake for Climate* [43]
Resilient Infrastructure in Latin America and the Caribbean, Inter-American Development
Bank, http://dx.doi.org/10.18235/0002049.

WBCSD (2018), *Natural Infrastructure Case Study: Izta-Popo – Replenishing Groundwater* [25]
through Reforestation in Mexico, World Business Council for Sustainable Development,
https://www.naturalinfrastructureforbusiness.org/wp-
content/uploads/2015/11/Volkswagen_NI4BizCaseStudy_Itza-Popo.pdf.

World Bank (2018), "Championing adaptation in Mexico: Protecting communities from the [52]
impacts of climate change", webpage, The World Bank, Washington, DC,
https://www.worldbank.org/en/results/2018/07/25/promover-la-adaptacion-en-mexico.

Zúñiga, E. and V. Magaña (2018), "Vulnerability and risk to intense rainfall in Mexico: The effect [19]
of land use cover change", *Investigaciones Geograficas*, Vol. 95,
http://dx.doi.org/10.14350/rig.59465.

Annex 2.A. List of stakeholders interviewed

The OECD undertook interviews with representatives from the following institutions in July 2020.

Table 2.A.1. Name of institutions

CENAPRED	National Center for Prevention of Disasters *Centro Nacional de Prevención de Desastres*
CONAFOR	National Forestry Commission Comisión Nacional Forestal
CONAGUA	National Water Commission Comisión Nacional del Agua
CONANP	National Commission of Natural Protected Areas Comisión Nacional de Áreas Naturales Protegidas
CONAZA	National Commission of Arid Zones Comisión Nacional de las Zonas Aridas
DGPCC	General Directorate of Policies for Climate Change Dirección General de Políticas para el Cambio Climático
INECC	National Institute of Ecology and Climate Change Instituto Nacional de Ecología y Cambio Climático
SHCP	Ministry of Finance and Public Credit Secretaría de Hacienda y Crédito Público
UNAM	National Autonomous University of Mexico Universidad Nacional Autónoma de México

The representatives interviewed were: Juan Carlos Centeno Álvarez, Cintia Amezcua, Angel Arias, Alfredo Araujo Beltrán, Miguel Angel Gallegos Benítez, Francisco Escobar Bravo, Luisa Buenrostro, Rodolfo Silva Casarín, Américo de la Garza Castellanos, Alejandro Cruz Castellón, Dra. Margarita Caso Chávez, Laurent Courty, Gloria Cuevas, Pilar Jacobo Enciso, Jorge Luis Nieves Frausto, Ricardo Prieto González, Salvador Espinosa Hernández, Jorge Zavala Hidalgo, Griselda Medina Laguna, María Fernanda Montero Lara, Amalia Salgado López, Malinali Dominguez Mares, Martin Ibarra Ochoa, Jesús Heriberto Montes Ortiz, Abril Salgado Paz, Lucía Guadalupe Matías Ramírez, Fabián Vázquez Romaña, Irma Karina López Sánchez, Homey Bon Santoyo, Juan Carlos Ramos Soto, Isabel María Hernández Toro, Cecilia Izcapa Treviño and Aseneth Ureña.

Notes

[1] For the purpose of this study, the term NbS encompasses a range of ecosystem-based management approaches such as ecosystem-based adaptation, ecosystem-based disaster risk reduction and green infrastructure. Water-related climate risks are scoped as flooding, which includes coastal, riverine and urban floods, as well as associated hazards caused by too much water, such as landslides; as well as drought.

[2] Examples of these water-related hazards include tropical cyclones, floods, landslides, avalanches and drought.

[3] Not yet adopted by February 2020, and based on information from interviews.

3. Managing water-related climate risks with nature-based solutions in the United Kingdom

This chapter presents the findings of a case study carried out in the United Kingdom on scaling up the use of nature-based solutions to address water-related climate risks. Building on the initial policy framework developed, it presents insights into the United Kingdom's enabling environment for nature-based solutions, specifically with regard to policy, governance and regulatory frameworks, as well as technical capacity and funding for nature-based solutions. It presents challenges the United Kingdom is confronted with as well as evolving good practices to address them.

3.1. Introduction

3.1.1. Context and objective of the case study

Healthy ecosystems and their associated services can provide effective protection against climaterelated variability and extremes. Nature-based solutions (NbS)[1] have recently gained momentum as measures that can protect, sustainably manage and restore nature, with the goal of preserving and enhancing ecosystem services to help address societal goals. For example, restoring a wetland can enhance its water storage capacity, thereby reducing flood risk in neighbouring communities, contributing to better water quality and enhancing species' habitats. NbS can be used as an alternative or complement to service provision through engineered, grey infrastructure. NbS tend to perform well across a wide range of conditions, and provide diverse benefits, making them particularly well-suited for adapting to a changing and uncertain climate (OECD, 2020[1]).

Recent OECD work on NbS has shown that despite their benefits in managing water-related climate risks, a number of bottlenecks, notably related to governance, regulations, policies and financing, hinder their uptake (OECD, 2020[1]). This chapter is one of a series of country case studies that explore existing challenges and aim to identify potential ways to overcome them. This case study provides an overview of the actors and institutions, policies, regulations, technical capacity, and financing which make up the enabling environment for water-related climate risk management in the United Kingdom. It is intended to share best practices and support policy makers in OECD countries in levelling the playing field for NbS. The series of case studies explores the following questions:

- How are NbS mainstreamed into planning and investment decisions for managing water-related climate risks?
- What tools and mechanisms are used to promote NbS?

3.1.2. Overview: Water-related climate risks

The United Kingdom has a temperate climate and diverse ecosystems, including woodlands, moorlands, heathlands, wetlands and coastal zones, which are home to rich biodiversity and provide additional services of high value to society, such as carbon sequestration and water filtration, as well as protection against climate-related risks, including drought and flooding (European Commission and European Environment Agency, 2011[2]; ONS, 2019[3]).

The United Kingdom is subject to a number of water-related climate risks, not least because of its long coastlines, extensive floodplains and high population density, many of which will be exacerbated by climate change. Although it has a relatively temperate climate characterised by year-round rainfall, climate change is expected to drive slight reductions in annual average rainfall in the coming decades, with seasonal distribution of rainfall expected to change with increased rainfall in the winter and decreased rainfall in the summer (OECD, 2013[4]). Extended periods of extreme rainfall are more likely to happen in the future, potentially resulting in increased risks of both fluvial and pluvial flooding by mid-century and an increase in the frequency and severity of floods even outside of recognised flood risk areas (CCC, 2017[5]).

The United Kingdom's sea level has risen at a best-estimate rate of 1.4 mm per year since 1901, which is close to the estimated rate for global sea level (CCC, 2017[5]). Compared to averages between 1981 and 2000, and depending on emission scenarios, the sea level near London is projected to rise between 0.25 metres and 1.15 metres between 2000 and 2100 (Met Office, 2019[6]). This will exacerbate coastal flood risk, as well as accelerate the process of coastal erosion, further threatening already exposed coastal communities (CCC, 2017[5]).

It is expected that many catchments will be experiencing water deficits by 2050, ultimately leading to increased competition among sectors for this resource. Furthermore, severe heatwaves are expected to occur more frequently (CCC, 2017[5]).

Water-related risks have already produced significant social and economic damages and losses in the United Kingdom. For example, the total direct costs of flooding in England between 2002 and 2013 amounted to EUR 23 billion. The 2007 floods were particularly severe and caused approximately EUR 4.4 billion in damage (Ellis and Lundy, 2016[7]). Approximately one in six properties in England are at risk of flooding from rivers or the sea (European Commission, 2017[8]). While the examples in this case study mainly cover flood risk management, water scarcity risk exists and can translate into high economic costs. For instance, providing emergency water during a drought was estimated to be between GBP 25 billion and GBP 40 billion, in addition to the environmental and public health impacts associated with emergency response (NIC, 2018[9]).

3.2. The enabling environment for managing water-related climate risks with nature-based solutions

3.2.1. Actors and institutional arrangements

Responsibility for managing water-related risks in the United Kingdom is shared among many public and private actors and bodies at the national and subnational levels across England, Northern Ireland, Scotland and Wales (Figure 3.1). The stakeholder groups play a different role in each stage of the policy and NbS project life cycles, from planning to implementation and maintenance as well as different governance levels, including at the catchment levels.[2] Key actors for implementation and maintenance include local risk management authorities (RMAs) who work in partnership to deliver flood risk management (Box 3.1).

Figure 3.1. Multi-level governance mapping of water-related risks in the United Kingdom

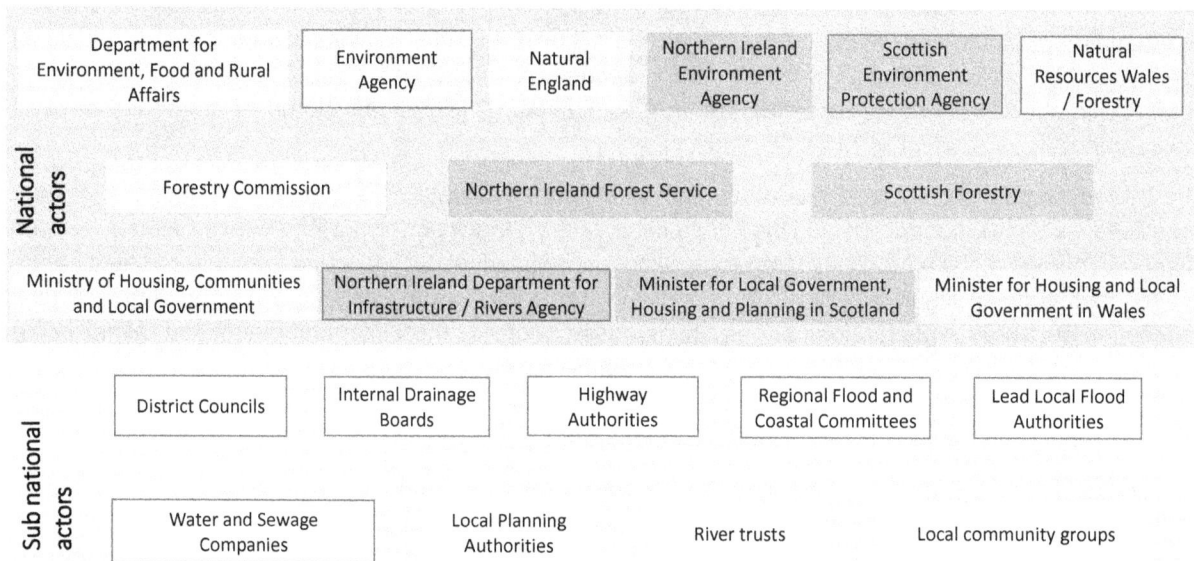

Notes: Actors responsible for setting the framework in England (light grey boxes), in Northern Ireland (dark blue boxes), in Scotland (dark grey boxes) and in Wales (light blue boxes). White boxes = actors responsible for implementation; red borders = risk management authorities. Rivers trusts can be found at the national level (The Rivers Trust) as well as the subnational level with 62 local rivers trusts in England. Forestry and Land Scotland plays a land manager role, whereas Scottish Forestry develops policies. The Department for Environment, Food & Rural Affairs focuses on projects in England and works closely with regional administrations in Northern Ireland, Scotland and Wales.

The Department for Environment, Food & Rural Affairs (Defra) plays a key role in promoting NbS for water-related climate risks. While Defra focuses on projects in England, it works closely with regional administrations in Northern Ireland, Scotland and Wales. It develops policies on water resources, including flooding, coastal erosion and drought, that are then implemented by RMAs at both the national, regional and local levels (Box 3.1). In addition, Defra plans and funds projects related to the use of NbS, such as through its Natural Flood Management (NFM) Programme (Defra, 2017[10]).

In England, the Environment Agency (EA), which plans, develops, manages, implements, funds and works with other stakeholders, is a non-departmental public body funded by Defra. It is responsible for environmental regulation and monitoring (it regulates water and air quality and waste management) and stakeholders need to engage with the EA to obtain environmental permits. The EA has an oversight role to steer flood risk management across England and is responsible for operational planning for managing flood, coastal erosion and drought risk. In addition, as a lead RMA, the EA specifies the responsibilities of other RMAs in England. Equivalents of the EA in Northern Ireland, Scotland and Wales are the Northern Ireland Environment Agency, the Scottish Environment Protection Agency (SEPA) and Natural Resources Wales. For instance, flood warning services are operated by SEPA in Scotland, Natural Resources Wales in Wales and the Environment Agency in England.

Box 3.1. Risk management authorities for managing floods, coastal erosion and droughts in England

The 2010 Flood and Water Management Act requires the Environment Agency to identify risk management authorities (RMAs) and specify their functions. The RMAs are required to share data and information and to co-operate with each other in order to effectively and efficiently carry out projects. The RMAs, which are mainly local and regional actors, include:

- Lead local flood authorities (e.g. a city or county council) are responsible for creating, implementing and maintaining strategies for local flood risk management in their respective regions (generally surface water and ordinary watercourses), for groundwater, as well as for creating and maintaining a flood risk assets register. They also play a key role in emergency planning and recovery after a flood event.

- District councils work closely with lead local flood authorities to manage local flood risk, as well as carry out flood risk management for ordinary watercourses. District councils in coastal regions can also act as coastal erosion management authorities.

- Internal drainage boards are independent public bodies that are responsible for water management at the local catchment level. They cover both water management reliant on gravitational flows as well as those requiring pumping.

- England's 12 regional flood and coastal committees are responsible for identifying and managing any coastal erosion or flood risk along coastlines or across catchments. Additionally, they promote effective investment for managing coastal erosion and floods and act as a link between authorities responsible for flood risk management.

- Highways authorities (e.g. Highways England) are responsible for managing highway drainage and roadside ditches.

Sources: Government of the United Kingdom (2010[11]; 2009[12]); Defra and Environment Agency (2015[13]).

Natural England a non-departmental public body funded by Defra that acts as the government's advisor for environmental topics, specifically for protecting the country's nature and landscapes in England. It provides advice and guidance on NFM measures, in particular to farmers involved with Countryside

Stewardship,[3] and frequently undertakes research on how NbS can be used to reduce flood and coastal erosion risks, and how droughts affect key ecosystems and species (Defra, 2020[14]; Natural England, n.d.[15]).

The Forestry Commission plans, develops, manages and funds projects. It is composed of Forest Services, the government's expert forestry advisors; Forestry England, which manages the public forest estate in England; and Forest Research, which delivers forestry and tree-related research for England, Scotland and Wales. It is responsible for the management and conservation of England's woodlands. For example, the Forestry Commission provided technical support to farmers and land managers for identifying areas where woodland planting would be most effective for managing pluvial and riverine flooding and limiting pollution and sediments reaching streams and rivers as part of the Woodlands for Water project. This was a joint project with the EA to reduce flood risk and improve water quality in the regions of Yorkshire and North East England (Environment Agency and Forestry Commission, 2019[16]). Equivalents of the Forestry Commission are the Northern Ireland Forest Service, Scottish Forestry and Natural Resources Wales.[4]

Finally, the Ministry of Housing, Communities and Local Government is a national government body that is responsible for setting policies and providing guidance for local planning authorities to ensure that flood risks are properly considered in planning processes. It encourages the uptake of NbS in its National Policy Planning Framework by recommending that local authorities consider the use of NFM in new property or infrastructure development projects, when appropriate (MHCLG, 2019[17]). Developers, which are required to consult local planning authorities regarding flood risks for new housing, infrastructure and community facilities, are advised to take appropriate action to avoid increasing flood risks and building on flood plains. The Northern Ireland Housing Executive; the Minister for Local Government, Housing and Planning in Scotland; and the Minister for Housing and Local Government in Wales have key roles to play in relation to housing, building standards and planning.

A large share of the land in the United Kingdom is privately owned and allocated to agricultural activities, making landowners, especially farmers, key stakeholders for managing water-related climate risks with NbS. The government is considering incentivising non-governmental stakeholders to implement NbS with payments against outcomes (e.g. allowing a private piece of land to be flooded for broader flood prevention benefits) and compensating them for potential trade-offs (e.g. potentially reducing agricultural output in the short term). Nonetheless, the process of successfully engaging landowners in NbS projects remains complex, due to a lack of clarity on responsibilities for the long-term operation and maintenance of NbS projects, funding and liability if NbS approaches ultimately fail or do not achieve their targeted goals. Establishing early and regular positive engagement with farmers and landowners helps to facilitate co-operation (Defra, 2020[14]).

Water companies in England and Wales are responsible for managing flood risk for surface water and sewer systems, as well as flood risks from the failure of their infrastructure. They manage public water supplies and associated drought risk (Environment Agency, 2017[18]). They are also notable landowners, which has facilitated the implementation and funding of NbS projects on their own land and has helped them become forerunners for NbS. Water companies in England and Wales have been involved in the implementation of NbS on third-party land, to cost-effectively accomplish water retention and improve water quality.

Other stakeholders such as non-governmental organisations (NGOs) (e.g. The Rivers Trust, wildlife trusts, charities [e.g. National Trust, Woodland Trust]) and community groups are also involved in the implementation of NbS projects and may act as a liaison between the government and landowners (Box 3.2). Some of these organisations, such as the National Trust or the Royal Society for the Protection of Birds, are also significant landowners. Flood action groups, which gather volunteers to represent their communities in reducing flood risk, have the potential to advocate for the implementation of NbS. Engaging with them can support awareness raising and capacity building of stakeholders on the benefits of NbS for flood prevention in specific regional catchments (Short et al., 2019[19]).

Box 3.2. The importance of working with stakeholders for successfully developing, managing and implementing nature-based solutions projects

The Tweed Forum, an organisation that works to enhance and restore the River Tweed (England and Scotland) catchment, has been instrumental in implementing nature-based solutions (NbS) initiatives and engaging with a variety of stakeholders to deliver lasting impacts. For example, through the Eddleston Water Project, this organisation has worked to restore natural landscapes, re-meander channels, create 30 new wetlands and plant over 300 000 trees in the area on 20 different farm units. During the process, the Tweed Forum collaborated with the Scottish Environment Protection Agency (SEPA) to engage with local stakeholders, including the community, business groups, landowners and farmers (Tweed Forum, 2020[20]; European Union, 2020[21]).

In addition to the Eddleston Water Project, the Tweed Forum is working with SEPA to help restore over five kilometres of Upper Nith (south-west Scotland) in order to reconnect the river with its floodplain and allow its natural features to be restored. In order to accomplish this, both the Tweed Forum and SEPA have worked with key landowners and the local community regarding the design of the project.

Source: Tweed Forum (n.d.[22]).

3.2.2. Policies and regulatory frameworks

Policies, strategies and plans

The United Kingdom has integrated and promoted NbS in its policy framework to reduce water-related risks as a complement to grey infrastructure (Huq and Stubbings, 2015[23]). Back in 2004, Defra promoted the creation of wetlands and washlands to address water-related climate risks in its "Making Space for Water" strategy (Defra, 2004[24]). The independent "Pitt Review", commissioned in the aftermath of major flood events in 2007, specifically recommended that Defra, the EA and Natural England develop catchment flood management plans and shoreline management plans, with a focus on NFM approaches (Box 3.3) (Ellis and Lundy, 2016[7]; Pitt, 2008[25]). The United Kingdom has promoted NbS in different sectors for flood protection, water quality management and climate change mitigation. Notably, Defra's Flood and Coastal Erosion Risk Management: Policy Statement prioritises the use of NbS and provides high-level policy support in favour of these approaches (Defra, 2020[26]). Table 3.1 provides an overview of national strategies and legislation related to environmental issues that support NbS and specifically address flood and drought risks. It is worth noting that NbS are not just supported in policies related to the environment, but also in sectoral policies pertaining to agriculture and water.

Box 3.3. Managing flood risks with natural flood management measures

The United Kingdom has increasingly promoted the use of nature-based solutions (NbS), notably for managing flood risks through so-called natural flood management (NFM) measures. These measures, which are a type of NbS, aim to emulate, protect or restore natural functions to reduce flooding and coastal erosion. The concepts of NbS and NFM have been gaining prominence in policy, as reflected in recent policy documents, such as Defra's Flood and Coastal Erosion Risk Management: Policy Statement, the National Flood and Coastal Erosion Risk Management Strategy for England, and the Natural England Action Plan.

Sources: Environment Agency (2017[27]; 2020[28]); Natural England (2020[29]).

The 25 Year Environment Plan, a key overarching policy document, focuses on restoring, maintaining and managing the natural capital assets to effectively reduce flood risk and coastal erosion in England. It also defines targets for water bodies to reach good environmental status and ensuring flow for ecological services (Defra, 2018[30]). The 2020 National Flood and Coastal Erosion Risk Management Strategy for England promotes measures such as sustainable drainage systems (SuDS)[5], restoring functions of river and floodplains and creating wetlands; it specifically supports the use of NbS that take a catchment-based approach[6] to manage both flood and drought risk. The National Planning Policy Framework calls for NFM techniques, specifically SuDS, to be considered by developers and local authorities during planning processes (MHCLG, 2019[17]; Environment Agency, 2020[28]). The 2020 National Framework for Water Resources makes clear that regional water resource management plans must consider wider resilience benefits. In this context, five regional groups were set up to develop regional plans for England (Environment Agency, 2020[31]).

Table 3.1. Selected bills and policies with relevance to nature-based solutions in the United Kingdom

	Name of (year)	Relevance to NbS
BILLS	UK Environment Bill (2019)	Contains measures to protect and restore natural habitats, improve water and air quality, and provide a net increase in the country's biodiversity.
	UK Agriculture Act (2019-21)	Contains measures to financially support landowners (e.g. farmers) for protecting ecosystems and implementing natural approaches to improve air and water quality in a new land management system.
POLICIES	25 Year Environment Plan (2018)	Promotes nature-based solutions measures such as natural flood management (NFM), woodland restoration and creation, sustainable urban drainage systems (SuDS), and peatland restoration in England.
	National Adaptation Programme and the Third Strategy for Climate Adaption Reporting (2018)	Sets objectives related to NFM, habitat restoration, peatland restoration and woodland restoration.
	National Planning Policy Framework (2019)	States that planning policies and decisions should help to preserve the natural environment by promoting the conservation and restoration of priority habitats and ecosystems, as well as incorporate NFM when appropriate.
	Defra's Flood and Coastal Erosion Risk Management: Policy Statement (2020)	Provides high-level policy support to the use of nature-based solutions.
	National Flood and Coastal Erosion Risk Management Strategy for England (2020)	Emphasises the need to use NFM when possible, including measures such as restoring natural flood plains, planting trees and the implementation of SuDS.
	National Strategy for Flood and Coastal Erosion Risk Management for Wales (2020)	Emphasises the need to use NFM when possible, including measures such as restoring natural flood plains, planting trees and the implementation of SuDS.

Sources: Defra (2020[32]; 2020[33]; 2018[30]; 2018[34]; 2020[26]); MHCLG (2019[17]); Environment Agency (2020[28]); Ministry for Environment, Energy and Rural Affairs (2020[35]).

To demonstrate its commitment in pursuing the use of NbS, England set several targets it seeks to reach as part of its 25 Year Environment Plan. Although they were not always established with the purpose of managing water-related risks but rather for mitigating climate change, they can provide co-benefits that contribute to the management of water-related risks. The targets include, for example, the restoration of 75% of 1 million hectares of terrestrial and freshwater protected sites or the increase of England's woodland to a 12% cover by 2060 (Defra, 2018[30]; 2019[36]).

Legal and regulatory frameworks

The regulatory environment has a powerful influence on the opportunity and feasibility of using NbS. The revised National Policy Planning Framework, which sets out the government's planning policies and how these are expected to be applied, provides an important push in support of green infrastructure. It specifically encourages local authorities, which are in charge of developing local planning policies and of granting construction licences and permits through which they can promote the use of NbS, to maintain and enhance green infrastructure. It also specifically encourages developers to incorporate NFM techniques to address water-related risks in new housing and other developments when these approaches are appropriate (MHCLG, 2019[17]). Specifically on forest management, the United Kingdom defined requirements and guidelines for sustainable forest management in its UK Forestry Standard, which regulates forestry and includes specific requirements to avoid an increased risk of flooding. It also considers how a woodland creation project can contribute to flood risk management (Forestry Commission, 2020[37]).

There are challenges that remain due to the inherent (and perceived) complexity of legal processes and the variety of land- and resource-use regulations for implementing NbS. The United Kingdom relies on specific planning tools such as catchment flood plans, shoreline plans and water level plans, general land-use planning and damage liability rules for managing flood risk. Case study interviewees flagged the difficulty of navigating the variety of local flood risk management strategies developed by lead local flood authorities. An additional issue concerns legal ownership and accountability. The lack of understanding regarding who is responsible for NbS projects over time proves to be an obstacle: landowners, and those leasing land, are often concerned over liability for potential maintenance, damage to land and a loss of control of their land. Therefore, it is important that risks and responsibilities are clearly identified and when appropriate, the government can step in to take on liability (Defra, 2020[14]). NbS are by nature often considered at a landscape or catchment scale and therefore involve a number of stakeholders and require significant multi-stakeholder collaboration.

These complexities stem from the need for NbS projects to reflect context specificities. In practice, this need translates into additional time, costs and resources to adequately prepare the assessments for implementing NbS projects. Local authorities rely on having the right information for their decision-making processes, particularly when assessments (e.g. environmental impact assessment or cost-benefit analysis of proposed flood risk reduction measures and financing options) are required (Defra and Environment Agency, 2014[38]). Defra underlines the uncertain costs and flood risk management benefits of NbS and the high modelling costs of these measures (Defra, 2020[14]). For example, large public investment infrastructure projects are appraised on the basis of cost-benefit analysis, which requires monetised data points. Difficult-to-monetise benefits – such as many of the co-benefits generated by NbS – may be under- or not valued at all (Defra, 2019[39]). While cost-benefit analysis can be difficult to undertake with NbS types of projects, several studies have attempted to quantify the benefits of NbS, some of which are highlighted in Box 3.4. Case study interviewees noted that this complexity can have high transaction costs, leading to grey infrastructure solutions being favoured due to the perceived "greater guarantee" of flood risk management benefits.

Box 3.4. Making the economic case for using nature-based solutions to address flood risk

A growing number of studies are making the economic case for incorporating nature-based solutions (NbS) to address flood risks in the United Kingdom. For example, London's "urban forest" of over 8.5 million trees is estimated to provide approximately EUR 3 million worth of flood mitigation benefits annually. Similarly, a modelling study showed that the installation of NbS approaches along the River Deben (Suffolk) could save up to 31% annually in average damages to both farmland and properties. The Research Agency of the Forestry Commission estimated the value of the flood regulation service provided by forests in Great Britain to range between GPB 92.7 million per year for summer-type floods and GPB 344.2 million per year for winter-type floods. Nonetheless, many co-benefits such as in terms of human health and biodiversity remain difficult to quantify and are delivered over a long-term time frame, which makes it challenging to integrate into existing methods to assess, value or monitor projects.

Sources: Treeconomics (2015[40]); Environment Agency (2017[27]); Broadmeadow et al. (2018[41]).

3.2.3. Tools and technical capacity

A solid knowledge and information base on the types and uses of NbS helps raise awareness about NbS as an alternative to grey solutions. Significant efforts have been undertaken to improve the information base on NbS, as noted by the case study interviewees. To that end, Defra requires the NbS pilot projects it funds to produce monitoring information that can then be used to strengthen the evidence base and develop context-specific information (e.g. the degree to which NbS can increase aquifer recharge to address drought risks can vary).

A range of other tools and guidance work are available to practitioners to share best practice and support NbS project-level implementation (Table 3.2). For example, the United Kingdom's experience with NbS has been recently summarised in the Evidence Directory, which draws together examples from over 60 successful NbS case studies to share good practices and lessons, as well as analysis of cost-benefit ratios, amongst flood risk management practitioners and other responsible bodies. This experience has helped to identify the current state of knowledge about the effectiveness of these measures (Environment Agency, 2017[42]).

Table 3.2. Guidance and toolboxes to support nature-based solutions practitioners

Source (year)	Name	Content	Target audience
Environment Agency (2017[42])	Working with Natural Processes Evidence Directory	Over 60 case studies on how to work with natural processes.	Practitioners
SEPA (2015[43])	SEPA Natural Flood Management Handbook	A practical guide to implement natural flood management (NFM) techniques for flood reduction.	Practitioners
Cbec (2017[44])	Natural Flood Management Toolbox	A practical guide on how to develop an NFM scheme.	Practitioners and communities
Yorkshire Dales National Park Authority, Yorkshire Dales Rivers Trust and North Yorkshire County Council (2017[45])	Natural Flood Management Measures: A Practical Guide for Upland Farmers	A practical guide on NFM measures.	Farmers and landowners
Environment Agency (2016[46])	How to Model and Map Catchment Processes When Flood Risk Management Planning	Review of the modelling software and associated data used for flood risk. management.	Practitioners
CIRIA (forthcoming[47])	Natural Flood Management Manual	A practical guide on the design, planning, implementation and maintenance of NFM measures.	Landowners/managers, community groups and environmental non-governmental organisations

Sources: Environment Agency (2018[48]; 2016[46]); SEPA (2015[43]); Cbec (2017[44]); Cumbria Strategic Flood Partnership (2017[49]); CIRIA (2018[50]).

3.2.4. Funding and finance

While there is no comprehensive estimate of the level of public and private investment in NbS in the United Kingdom, case study interviewees find that it appears to be steadily increasing in line with policy priorities, remaining though at a much lower level than funding for grey infrastructure, which reaches several billions of euros.

Public funding is an important source of finance to kick-start and cover any risks that may arise from NbS projects. A number of public funding sources are available for NbS (Table 3.3). The United Kingdom's 2020 Budget allocates EUR 710 million to the Nature for Climate Fund to support the creation, restoration and management of woodland and peatland habitats, plant more than 40 million trees ,and restore 35 000 hectares of peatland in England. EUR 33 million of it has been brought forward as part of the EUR 88 million Green Recovery Challenge Fund to make funds readily available. Projects funded in Round 1 will restore woodland, peatland and wetland habitats and plant over 800 000 trees by March 2022.

Defra provides the majority of its funding for flood and coastal erosion risk management projects, including for NbS, to the EA as grant-in-aid.[7] The EA spends the funding directly on managing flood risk, but it also passes some of this funding on as capital grants for flood or coastal erosion defence improvements to local authorities or internal drainage boards. The rules defining the level of the grant payment were revised in 2020 to better reflect wider environmental benefits (Defra, 2019[39]; 2020[14]; Environment Agency, 2020[51]).

Public funding is sometimes channelled through or complemented by NGOs, philanthropies, communities or private companies (such as property developers or water companies), as it is acknowledged that multiple actors derive different benefits from an NbS and can potentially co-fund an NbS. The government encourages NGOs to implement NbS projects against flood risks through Defra's NFM Programme that dedicates half of its funding to NGO-led projects. Since 2017, Defra has allocated over EUR 16 million to projects across England for natural flood defences. Over 50 individual projects, including for restoring floodplains and planting of trees, have been supported (Defra, 2017[10]). Many NbS projects benefit from grant funding and donations (e.g. EU funding,[8] public grants or subsidies, philanthropic contributions, crowdfunding) to support efforts such as education, training, awareness raising, project support and monitoring. Box 3.5 shows that partners are joining forces to find innovative financing solutions for NbS.

In addition, the United Kingdom incentivises landowners, farmers and foresters to implement actions on private land (e.g. planting woodlands, hedge planting or floodplain restoration) that deliver environmental benefits such as improved water quality, climate change mitigation and flood management. These schemes, among others, include the Environmental Land Management[9] and the Countryside Stewardship schemes (Defra and Natural England, 2019[52]; Defra, 2020[53]). Support to woodland creation has enhanced payment rates (e.g. the English Woodland Grant Scheme) or is targeted to priority catchments to deliver flood risk management benefits or to provide riparian shade to maintain lower water temperatures (e.g. the Countryside Stewardship).

Woodland creation projects that contribute to flood risk management can leverage government funding through the Woodland Carbon Code and the Woodland Carbon Guarantee, a government incentive. They mainly aim to further develop domestic carbon markets and are not explicitly aimed at flood risk management.[10]

As noted by case study interviewees, the availability of funding for monitoring and maintenance remains an issue for project implementation. This can lead to wariness amongst landholders, as they do not want to bind themselves to potentially costly long-term maintenance or unknown expenses in the case of an NbS project's failure. Funders are concerned over uncertainty surrounding the duration of a scheme, maintenance obligations, the availability of future funding, possibilities to demonstrate the value and the effectiveness of NbS installed by third parties (Defra, 2020[14]). Monitoring is now a requirement for projects funded under Defra NFM Programme.

Table 3.3. Examples of public funding mechanisms and sources available for nature-based solutions in the United Kingdom

Type	Name	Description
Programmes and funds	Flood and Coastal Resilience Innovation Programme	Between 2021 and 2027, the programme will allocate a share of the budget (EUR 168 million) to 25 local areas (e.g. county, city, town, village, a river catchment, a tidal estuary or part of the coast) for projects demonstrating how practical innovative actions improve resilience to flooding and coastal erosion. It is part of the broader programme of EUR 5.8 billion to protect over 300 000 properties in England. **Budget**: EUR 225 million
	Defra NFM Programme	Funds projects to implement natural flood defences and spur innovation. While many projects are planned and implemented by the national government, part of the funding has been given to local stakeholders and third sector organisations. **Budget**: EUR 16.5 million
	Nature for Climate Fund	Set up by Defra to plant 40 million trees and restore over 30 000 hectares of peatland in England. **Budget**: EUR 710 million
	Natural Environment Impact Fund	To stimulate private investment and market-based mechanisms. **Budget**: EUR 11 million
Other funding mechanisms	Local flood levy funding	A type of tariff raised by the Environment Agency, placed on local authorities, and subject to the approval of regional flood and coastal committees, which can be used for nature-based solutions projects.
	Local authority capital	Specific capital grants can be used to fund the expenditure for which they have been set, e.g. flood risk management works.
	Reverse auction initiatives	Landowners to bid on funding for implementing measures, such as the creation of leaky dams, hedge planting and maize management: – EnTrade (EUR 1.4 million contracted) – Somerset Reverse NFM Auction
	Countryside Stewardship Facilitation Fund*	Provides funding to local communities and organisations on the understanding that they are bringing together different stakeholders to improve the local environment, primarily landowners and farmers.
	Environmental Land Management Scheme*	Farmers, foresters and other land managers will be paid for managing their land in a way that will deliver against key 25 Year Environment Plan's goals.
	Funding sources relating to development and regeneration	Section 106 (S106) agreements and the Community Infrastructure Levy allow local authorities to charge developers a fee for new infrastructure works (including green spaces).
	Lotteries	Lotteries (e.g. Heritage Lottery Fund, Big Lottery, Arts Council) support projects that enhance the natural heritage of an area.

* Will be phased out and replaced by environmental land management schemes in 2024, which is designed to replace the EU's Common Agricultural Policy.
Sources: HM Treasury (2020[54]); Defra (2020[14]; 2020[55]); EnTrade (2020[56]); Environment Agency (2020[57]).

Despite different public funding sources being available for NbS projects, practitioners often face difficulties in accessing funding (Defra, 2020[14]). Complex application processes requiring modelling and the production of evidence impede access to certain funding. Case study interviewees also raised the challenge that innovative funding mechanisms often have a higher perception of risk and uncertainty due to their newness, which can hinder their use.

Public sources have proven to be important in mobilising additional private sources of finance, as it is often difficult to secure private financing and move towards a loan-based model for NbS projects due to the lack of clear revenue stream. Defra and the EA recently set up the natural environment Investment Readiness Fund, which will commit up to EUR 10 million to help prepare projects that could be suitable for commercial investment. The aim is to broaden the funding base with private sector investment in natural environment projects by stimulating a pipeline of projects that can generate revenue from ecosystem services and attract repayable investment (Environment Agency, 2020[58]).

To attract private financing for NbS, Defra, the EA, the Esmée Fairbairn Foundation and Triodos Bank UK joined forces to provide seed grants to four NbS pilot projects,[11] to be complemented by private funding. One of these projects, led by The Rivers Trust and United Utilities in partnership, aims to use NbS in the River Wyre catchment to reduce the frequency of flooding. To improve the business case, the private funds are to be reimbursed by the potential beneficiaries by the NbS project, which include a water company, the EA, local authorities, the insurance industry, locally based businesses and homeowners (The Flood Hub, n.d.[61]).

There are examples of fully privately funded NbS projects, indicating that a business can be made. For example, water companies (e.g. Scottish Water, Anglian Water, Severn Trent) financed the creation of wetlands to address water pollution (Trémolet et al., 2019[62]). While there are several examples of privately funded NbS for addressing water pollution, privately funded NbS for flood and drought risks remain scarce.

Some water companies in England and Wales are financing NbS out of tariff revenues. Ofwat, the national water industry regulator, agreed to include an outcome-based payment in its tariff-setting formula linked to its environmental performance and specifically authorised these companies to use their revenues for such purposes. Severn Trent, for instance, invested its own resources gathered from water tariffs and mobilised matching funding from other sources, including European grant programmes (e.g. LIFE), public subsidies from the EA and farmers (Trémolet et al., 2019[62]).

References

Broadmeadow, S. et al. (2018), *Valuing Flood Regulation Services of Existing Forest to Inform Natural Capital Accounts*, Forest Research, https://www.forestresearch.gov.uk/documents/5499/Final_report_valuing_flood_regulation_services_051218.pdf. [41]

Cbec (2017), *Natural Flood Management Toolbox: Guidance for Working with Natural Processes in Flood Management Schemes*, Cbec, Inverness, Scotland, https://catchmentbasedapproach.org/wp-content/uploads/2018/08/EA-NFM-Toolbox-Final-Draft.compressed.pdf. [44]

CCC (2017), *UK Climate Change Risk Assessment 2017 – Synthesis Report: Priorities for the Next Five Years*, Committee on Climate Change, London, https://www.theccc.org.uk/wp-content/uploads/2016/07/UK-CCRA-2017-Synthesis-Report-Committee-on-Climate-Change.pdf. [5]

CIRIA (2018), "Guidance on natural flood management RP1094", webpage, Construction Industry Research and Information Association, https://www.ciria.org/Research/Projects_underway2/Guidance_on_natural_flood_management_RP1094.aspx. [50]

CIRIA (forthcoming), *Natural Flood Management Manual*, Construction Industry Research and Information Association, forthcoming. [47]

Cumbria Strategic Flood Partnership (2017), *Natural Flood Management Measures: A Practical Guide for Farmers*, Cumbria Strategic Flood Partnership, https://catchmentbasedapproach.org/wp-content/uploads/2018/11/North-West-NFM-handbook.pdf. [49]

Defra (2020), *Environment Bill 2020*, Department for Environment, Food & Rural Affairs, https://www.gov.uk/government/publications/environment-bill-2020. [32]

Defra (2020), *Flood and Coastal Erosion Risk Management: Policy Statement*, Department for Environment, Food & Rural Affairs, https://www.gov.uk/government/publications/flood-and-coastal-erosion-risk-management-policy-statement (accessed on 15 February 2021). [26]

Defra (2020), "New details of the flagship Environmental Land Management Scheme unveiled by Environment Secretary", *Defra in the Media Blog*, Department for Environment, Food & Rural Affairs, https://deframedia.blog.gov.uk/2020/02/25/new-details-of-the-flagship-environmental-land-management-scheme-unveiled-by-environment-secretary. [53]

Defra (2020), *The Agriculture Bill 2019-21*, Department for Environment, Food & Rural Affairs, https://commonslibrary.parliament.uk/research-briefings/cbp-8702. [33]

Defra (2020), *The Enablers and Barriers to the Delivery of Natural Flood Management Projects*, Department for Environment, Food & Rural Affairs, http://sciencesearch.defra.gov.uk/Document.aspx?Document=14754_FD2713_Final_Report.pdf. [14]

Defra (2020), *The Future for Food, Farming and the Environment: Policy Statement (2020)*, Department for Environment, Food & Rural Affairs, https://www.gov.uk/government/publications/the-future-for-food-farming-and-the-environment-policy-statement-2020. [55]

Defra (2019), *A Green Future: Our 25 Year Plan to Improve the Environment*, Department for Environment, Food & Rural Affairs, https://www.gov.uk/government/publications/25-year-environment-plan. [36]

Defra (2019), *Central Government Funding for Flood and Coastal Erosion Risk Management in England*, Department for Environment, Food & Rural Affairs, https://assets.publishing.service.gov.uk/government/uploads/system/uploads/attachment_data/file/877997/FCERM_Funding_Statistics_Publication_September_2019_accessv2.pdf. [39]

Defra (2018), *25 Year Environment Plan*, Department for Environment, Food & Rural Affairs, https://www.gov.uk/government/publications/25-year-environment-plan. [30]

Defra (2018), *The National Adaptation Programme and the Third Strategy for Climate Adaptation Reporting: Making the Country Resilient to a Changing Climate*, Department for Environment, Food & Rural Affairs, https://assets.publishing.service.gov.uk/government/uploads/system/uploads/attachment_data/file/727252/national-adaptation-programme-2018.pdf. [34]

Defra (2017), "Schemes across the country to receive £15 million of natural flood management funding", press release, Department for Environment, Food & Rural Affairs, https://www.gov.uk/government/news/schemes-across-the-country-to-receive-15-million-of-natural-flood-management-funding. [10]

Defra (2004), *Making Space for Water: Developing a New Government Strategy for Flood and Coastal Erosion Risk Management in England*, Department for Environment, Food & Rural Affairs, London, http://www.met.reading.ac.uk/~sws00rsp/teaching/postgrad/consultation[1].pdf. [24]

Defra and Environment Agency (2015), *Flood and Coastal Erosion: Risk Management Authorities*, Department for Environment, Food & Rural Affairs and Environment Agency, https://www.gov.uk/government/collections/flood-and-coastal-erosion-risk-management-authorities. [13]

Defra and Environment Agency (2014), "Local flood risk management strategies: Tools for support", webpage, Government of the United Kingdom, https://www.gov.uk/guidance/flood-risk-management-information-for-flood-risk-management-authorities-asset-owners-and-local-authorities#local-flood-risk-management-strategies-tools-for-support. [38]

Defra and Natural England (2019), *Agreement Holders' Information: Environmental Stewardship*, Government of the United Kingdom, https://www.gov.uk/guidance/environmental-stewardship. [52]

eftec, Environmental Finance and Countryscape (2019), *Greater Manchester Natural Capital Investment Plan*, eftec, London, https://naturegreatermanchester.co.uk/wp-content/uploads/2019/01/eftec-GM-NCIP-Summary-A4-16pp-v3-LoRes2.pdf. [59]

Ellis, J. and L. Lundy (2016), "Implementing sustainable drainage systems for urban surface water management within the regulatory framework in England and Wales", *Journal of Environmental Management*, Vol. 183/Pt 3, pp. 630-636, http://dx.doi.org/10.1016/j.jenvman.2016.09.022. [7]

EnTrade (2020), "A new deal for the natural environment", website, EnTrade, https://www.entrade.co.uk. [56]

Environment Agency (2020), *Flood and Coastal Resilience Innovation Programme*, Environment Agency, https://www.gov.uk/guidance/flood-and-coastal-resilience-innovation-programme. [57]

Environment Agency (2020), *Investment Readiness Fund*, Environment Agency, https://thefloodhub.co.uk/wp-content/uploads/2020/09/Natural-Environment-Investment-Readiness-Fund.pdf. [58]

Environment Agency (2020), *Meeting our Future Water Needs: A National Framework for Water Resources*, Environment Agency, Bristol, England, https://assets.publishing.service.gov.uk/government/uploads/system/uploads/attachment_data/file/873100/National_Framework_for_water_resources_summary.pdf. [31]

Environment Agency (2020), *National Flood and Coastal Erosion Risk Management Strategy for England*, Environment Agency, https://www.gov.uk/government/publications/national-flood-and-coastal-erosion-risk-management-strategy-for-england--2. [28]

Environment Agency (2020), *Operational Principles to Follow When Setting Up Funding Partnerships to Tackle Flood and Coastal Erosion*, Environment Agency, Bristol, England, https://assets.publishing.service.gov.uk/government/uploads/system/uploads/attachment_data/file/879973/Operational_Principles_for_FCERM_funding_partnerships.pdf. [51]

Environment Agency (2018), *Working with Natural Processes – Evidence Directory*, Environment Agency, https://assets.publishing.service.gov.uk/government/uploads/system/uploads/attachment_data/file/681411/Working_with_natural_processes_evidence_directory.pdf. [48]

Environment Agency (2017), *Drought Response: Our Framework for England*, Environment Agency, Bristol, England, https://assets.publishing.service.gov.uk/government/uploads/system/uploads/attachment_data/file/625006/LIT_10104.pdf. [18]

Environment Agency (2017), "Natural flood management – part of the nation's flood resilience", webpage, Environment Agency, https://www.gov.uk/government/news/natural-flood-management-part-of-the-nations-flood-resilience. [27]

Environment Agency (2017), *Working with Natural Processes to Reduce Flood Risk*, Environment Agency, https://www.gov.uk/government/publications/working-with-natural-processes-to-reduce-flood-risk. [42]

Environment Agency (2016), *How to Model and Map Catchment Processes When Flood Risk Management Planning*, Environment Agency, https://www.gov.uk/government/publications/how-to-model-and-map-catchment-processes-when-flood-risk-management-planning. [46]

Environment Agency and Forestry Commission (2019), "Reduce flood risk with the Woodlands for Water scheme", press release, Environment Agency and Forestry Commission, https://www.gov.uk/government/news/reduce-flood-risk-with-the-woodlands-for-water-scheme. [16]

European Commission (2017), *The EU Environmental Implementation Review 2019: Country Report United Kingdom*, European Commission, Brussels, http://ec.europa.eu/environment/eir/pdf/report_uk_en.pdf. [8]

European Commission and European Environment Agency (2011), *United Kingdom: Biodiversity Information System for Europe*, European Union. [2]

European Union (2020), "Finding common ground with farmers", webpage, European Union, https://building-with-nature.eu/about-building-nature/news/nieuwsberichten/2020/finding-common-ground-farmers. [21]

Forestry Commission (2020), *The UK Forestry Standard*, Government of the United Kingdom, https://assets.publishing.service.gov.uk/government/uploads/system/uploads/attachment_data/file/687147/The_UK_Forestry_Standard.pdf. [37]

Government of the United Kingdom (2010), *Flood and Water Management Act 2010*, Government of the United Kingdom, https://www.legislation.gov.uk/ukpga/2010/29/contents. [11]

Government of the United Kingdom (2009), *The Flood Risk Regulations 2009*, Government of the United Kingdom, https://www.legislation.gov.uk/uksi/2009/3042/contents/made. [12]

Greater Manchester Combined Authority (2020), "The IGNITION Project", webpage, Greater Manchester Combined Authority, https://www.greatermanchester-ca.gov.uk/what-we-do/environment/natural-environment/ignition. [60]

HM Treasury (2020), *Budget 2020: Delivering on Our Promises to the British People*, Government of the United Kingdom, https://assets.publishing.service.gov.uk/government/uploads/system/uploads/attachment_data/file/871799/Budget_2020_Web_Accessible_Complete.pdf. [54]

Huq, N. and A. Stubbings (2015), "How is the role of ecosystem services considered in local level flood management policies: Case study in Cumbria, England", *Journal of Environmental Assessment Policy and Management*, Vol. 17/04, http://dx.doi.org/10.1142/s1464333215500325. [23]

Met Office (2019), *UKCP18 Science Overview Report*, Met Office, London, https://www.metoffice.gov.uk/pub/data/weather/uk/ukcp18/science-reports/UKCP18-Overview-report.pdf. [6]

MHCLG (2019), *National Planning Policy Framework*, Ministry of Housing, Communities & Local Government, London, https://assets.publishing.service.gov.uk/government/uploads/system/uploads/attachment_data/file/810197/NPPF_Feb_2019_revised.pdf. [17]

Ministry for Environment, Energy and Rural Affairs (2020), *National Strategy for Flood and Coastal Erosion Risk Management (FCERM)*, Government of Wales, https://gov.wales/welsh-government-launches-its-national-strategy-flood-and-coastal-erosion-risk-management-fcerm. [35]

Natural England (2020), *Building Partnerships for Nature's Recovery: Action Plan 2020/21*, Natural England, https://assets.publishing.service.gov.uk/government/uploads/system/uploads/attachment_dat a/file/906289/natural-england-action-plan-2020-21.pdf. [29]

Natural England (n.d.), "About us", webpage, Natural England, https://www.gov.uk/government/organisations/natural-england/about. [15]

NIC (2018), *Preparing for a Drier Future: England's Water Infrastructure Needs*, National Infrastructure Commission, https://nic.org.uk/app/uploads/NIC-Preparing-for-a-Drier-Future-26-April-2018.pdf. [9]

OECD (2020), "Nature-based solutions for adapting to water-related climate risks", *OECD Environment Policy Papers*, No. 21, OECD Publishing, Paris, https://dx.doi.org/10.1787/2257873d-en. [1]

OECD (2013), *Water and Climate Change Adaptation: Policies to Navigate Uncharted Waters*, OECD Publishing, Paris, http://dx.doi.org/10.1787/9789264200449-en. [4]

ONS (2019), "UK natural capital accounts", Office for National Statistics, https://www.ons.gov.uk/economy/environmentalaccounts/bulletins/uknaturalcapitalaccounts/2 019#overview-of-uk-ecosystem-services (accessed on 25 August 2020). [3]

Pitt, S. (2008), *Pitt Review: Lessons Learned from the 2007 Floods*, Government of the United Kingdom, https://webarchive.nationalarchives.gov.uk/20100812084907/http://archive.cabinetoffice.gov. uk/pittreview/_/media/assets/www.cabinetoffice.gov.uk/flooding_review/pitt_review_full%20pd f.pdf. [25]

Poleto, C. and R. Tassi (2012), "Sustainable urban drainage systems", in Prof. Javaid, M. (ed.), *Drainage Systems*, pp. 55-72, Intech, Rijeka, Croatia, http://dx.doi.org/10.5772/34491. [64]

SEPA (2015), *Natural Flood Management Handbook*, Scottish Environment Protection Agency, Stirling, Scotland, https://www.sepa.org.uk/media/163560/sepa-natural-flood-management-handbook1.pdf. [43]

Short, C. et al. (2019), "Capturing the multiple benefits associated with nature-based solutions: Lessons from a natural flood management project in the Cotswolds, UK", *Land Degradation & Development*, Vol. 30/3, pp. 241-252, http://dx.doi.org/10.1002/ldr.3205. [19]

The Flood Hub (n.d.), *Wyre NFM Project*, The Flood Hub, https://thefloodhub.co.uk/wyre-nfm-project. [61]

Treeconomics (2015), *Valuing London's Urban Forest: Results of the London i-Tree Eco Project*, Treeconomics, London, https://www.london.gov.uk/sites/default/files/valuing_londons_urban_forest_i-tree_report_final.pdf. [40]

Trémolet, S. et al. (2019), *Investing in Nature for Europe Water Security*, The Nature Conservancy, Ecologic Institute and ICLEI, https://www.nature.org/content/dam/tnc/nature/en/documents/Investing_in_Nature_for_Europ ean_Water_Security_02.pdf. [62]

Tweed Forum (2020), "The Eddleston Water Project", webpage, Tweed Forum, https://tweedforum.org/our-work/projects/the-eddleston-water-project. [20]

Tweed Forum (n.d.), "Projects", webpage, Tweed Forum, https://tweedforum.org/our-work/current-projects/page/2. [22]

WWT (2018), "The catchment based approach: What is it and why does it matter?", webpage, Water & Wastewater Treatment, https://wwtonline.co.uk/features/the-catchment-based-approach-what-is-it-and-why-does-it-matter. [63]

Yorkshire Dales National Park Authority, Yorkshire Dales Rivers Trust and North Yorkshire County Council (2017), *Natural Flood Management Measures: A Practical Guide for Upland Farmers*, Yorkshire Dales National Park Authority, https://thefloodhub.co.uk/wp-content/uploads/2018/10/A-practical-guide-for-farmers.pdf. [45]

Annex 3.A. List of stakeholders interviewed

The OECD undertook interviews with representatives from the following institutions in September 2020.

Table 3.A.1. Name of institutions

Defra (Department for Environment, Food & Rural Affairs)
Environment Agency
Forestry Commission
Knepp Estate
Mott MacDonald
Natural England
Scottish Environmental Protection Agency
The Rivers Trust
Tweed Forum
Water Level Management Alliance

The representatives interviewed were: Daniel Barwick, Giles Bloomfield, Mark Broadmeadow, Lydia Burgess-Gamble, Luke Comins, Jason Emrich, Heather Forbes, Bethany Green, Jon Hollis, Ashley Holt, James Knightbridge, Russ Money, Matthew Philpot, Dan Turner, Orlando Venn and Emma Wren.

Notes

[1] For the purpose of this study, the term NbS encompasses a range of ecosystem-based management approaches such as ecosystem-based adaptation, ecosystem-based disaster risk reduction and green infrastructure. Water-related climate risks are scoped as flooding, which includes coastal, riverine and urban floods, as well as associated hazards caused by too much water, such as landslides; as well as drought.

[2] A catchment-based approach is defined as being a collaborative approach at the river catchment scale that brings together a range of local partners to deliver environmental improvements (WWT, 2018[63]).

[3] Countryside Stewardship is an agri-environment payment that provides financial incentives for farmers, woodland owners, foresters and land managers to look after and improve the environment. Although the scheme is not directly related to flooding, it promotes measures that are similar to those considered for NFM (see: https://www.gov.uk/government/collections/countryside-stewardship).

[4] When Natural Resources Wales took over responsibility for forestry in Wales in 2013, it brought together the work of the Countryside Council for Wales, Forestry Commission Wales and the Environment Agency in Wales, as well as some Welsh government functions.

[5] Sustainable urban drainage systems are defined as being systems that provide an alternative or complement to traditional drainage systems by efficiently managing the drainage of surface water in urban areas. Examples include permeable surfaces and green roofs (Poleto and Tassi, 2012[64]).

[6] A catchment-based approach is defined as being a collaborative approach at the river catchment scale that brings together a range of local partners to deliver environmental improvements (WWT, 2018[63]).

[7] Defra allocates central funding to flood and coastal erosion risk management projects through partnership funding which aims to share the costs between national and local sources of funding. This approach allows any worthwhile project (where benefits are greater than costs) to qualify for government money, known as grant-in-aid (Environment Agency, 2020[51]).

[8] Although the United Kingdom has left the European Union, EU funding that has already been awarded continues to be provided.
[9] This scheme is proposed under the Agricultural Act.

[10] https://www.woodlandcarboncode.org.uk and https://www.gov.uk/guidance/woodland-carbon-guarantee.

[11] Devon Wildlife Trust's restoration of the Caen wetlands; the Rivers Trust's work on natural flood management in the Wyre catchment in Lancashire; the National Farmers Union's work to reduce nitrate pollution in Poole Harbour; Moors for the Future Partnership's restoration and conservation of peatlands in the Pennines.